MultiChurch

Exploring the Future of Multisite

Brad House and
Gregg Allison

ZONDERVAN

MultiChurch
Copyright © 2017 by Gregg Allison and Brad House

This title is also available as a Zondervan ebook.

Requests for information should be addressed to:
Zondervan, *3900 Sparks Dr. SE, Grand Rapids, Michigan 49546*

ISBN 978-0-310-53053-4

Unless otherwise noted, Scripture quotations are taken from the Holy Bible, New International Version®, NIV®. Copyright © 1973, 1978, 1984, 2011 by Biblica, Inc.® Used by permission of Zondervan. All rights reserved worldwide. www.Zondervan .com. The "NIV" and "New International Version" are trademarks registered in the United States Patent and Trademark Office by Biblica, Inc.®

Scripture quotations marked ESV are from the ESV® Bible (The Holy Bible, English Standard Version®). Copyright © 2001 by Crossway, a publishing ministry of Good News Publishers. Used by permission. All rights reserved.

Any Internet addresses (websites, blogs, etc.) and telephone numbers in this book are offered as a resource. They are not intended in any way to be or imply an endorsement by Zondervan, nor does Zondervan vouch for the content of these sites and numbers for the life of this book.

All rights reserved. No part of this publication may be reproduced, stored in a retrieval system, or transmitted in any form or by any means—electronic, mechanical, photocopy, recording, or any other—except for brief quotations in printed reviews, without the prior permission of the publisher.

Cover Design: Studio Gearbox
Cover image: Shutterstock
Interior design: Kait Lamphere
Interior imagery: © Teamarwen/Shutterstock

Printed in the United States of America

HB 01.19.2022

If you're doing multisite or plan to in the future—*stop now* and read *MultiChurch*! Allison and House will save you thousands of dollars, and hours in multisite pain and dumb tax. In the process, they give a remedy to the multisite movement's greatest need—a theologically grounded and implication-rich response to multisite's most challenging questions. If you want to move past adding sites and venues to multiplying disciples, leaders, and churches, read *MultiChurch* and apply.

BRIAN FRYE, national collegiate strategist,
North American Mission Board

Gregg Allison and Brad House add valuable data and insight to the nascent research and critique of item multisite movement. It's an increasingly significant part of the local church landscape, and it's not going away anytime soon. Whether you are currently leading a multisite church, considering launching one, or attending one, this book will help you better understand the opportunities and challenges that come with a multisite ministry.

LARRY OSBORNE, pastor and author, North Coast Church, Vista, CA

Now in its third decade, the multisite movement began as a radical idea to solve church facility restrictions and has now become a mainstream strategy for all kinds of churches. The authors of *MultiChurch: Exploring the Future of Multisite* have served this movement well by describing its evolution, naming its distinct expressions, addressing its criticisms, and charting a course forward for a movement that is not slowing down and is continually morphing. Written by a seasoned multisite practitioner and a hands-on theologian, House and Allison address the multiple challenges of a multisite church and provide an invaluable roadmap for church leaders wherever they are on their multisite journey. This is a must-read book for multisite church leaders!

JIM TOMBERLIN, pastor, author, multisite pioneer, and consultant;
founder, MultiSite Solutions

Dr. Gregg Allison and Brad House have both helped shape my approach to ministry in unique ways. As the supervisor for my doctoral degree, Gregg pressed my theology of the church into consistent practice, and Brad taught me how to lead smaller communities in the context of a large, rapidly growing church. In *MultiChurch*, you will see the authors' respective complementary perspectives, as well as their distinctive theological and pastoral gifts on display. *MultiChurch* provides an excellent framework for continued discussion around the multisite church model, while maintaining a consistent doctrinal grounding in the discipline of ecclesiology. Finally, the book strikes a sound balance between helpful encouragement and honest critique of the ever-growing and changing landscape of church practice. I am convinced any leader in a multisite church will benefit from this book!

> **DR. TODD ENGSTROM**, executive pastor of ministry strategies,
> The Austin Stone Community Church

Frankly, I've been chilling on multi-site models. But Allison and House have reignited the topic in ways that are prescient and defrosting to one's iced-over imagination. *MultiChurch* bears weight too, knowing that the audience must find simplicity in the theological and ecclesiological complexities. Yet, Allison and House are at their best navigating between ambiguity and clarity, polity and missiology; and then gently escorting us to a perch from which we can glimpse "multichurch." If you are struggling with multisite models, polity perplexities, or how to take practical steps forward, get this book!

> **DAVE HARVEY**, executive director of Sojourn Network, teaching pastor
> at Summit Church in Naples, founder AmICalled.com, and author of
> *When Sinners Say I Do*; & *Letting Go: Rugged Love for Wayward Souls*
> (@RevDaveHarvey)

Gregg Allison and Brad House have written a thoughtful and helpful book for those who are seriously considering the future of multisite, which they call *MultiChurch*. As a pastor of a multisite church that has transitioned into a family of churches, I can say that what they have written here will be extremely helpful for those interested in wrestling with the theological and practical considerations involved in leading multiple congregations toward church health.

> **HARVEY TURNER**, founding pastor of Living Stones Churches,
> lead pastor of Living Stones Reno, Acts 29 US West Leadership Team

This is the book every pastor and elder team should read—whether they are currently leading or thinking about starting a multisite church. It's grounded in Scripture and highly practical. I am thrilled Brad and Gregg wrote this book. It's a gift to Jesus's Church.

> **ELLIOT GRUDEM**, founder and president, Leaders Collective

This book is dedicated to Sojourn Community Church. We are grateful for all the leaders who desire to cultivate a healthy, thriving church. And we are indebted to the members of Sojourn, who inspire us to find better ways to empower the church for the advancement of the kingdom of God.

Contents

Introduction • 9

1 • A Multichurch Evolution • 21

Section 1: Scouting

2 • Landscape • 31
3 • Landmarks • 45
4 • Landmines • 77
5 • The Future • 96

Section 2: Orienteering

6 • MultiOrg • 119
7 • MultiPolity • 143
8 • MultiMinistry • 160
9 • MultiMoney • 174
10 • MultiMembership • 185

Section 3: Setting Out

11 • Navigating Transition • 201
12 • The Rest of the Story • 217

Appendix I: Grievance Policy • 221
Appendix II: Micropolity • 224
Notes • 229

Introduction

> We have an unknown distance yet to run, an unknown river to
> explore. What falls there are, we know not; what rocks beset
> the channel, we know not; what walls ride over the river, we
> know not. Ah, well! we may conjecture many things.

JOHN WESLEY POWELL

John Wesley Powell was a pioneer. Today Powell is hailed as the first pioneer (of European decent) to explore the Grand Canyon, but in the latter half of the 1800s, Powell wasn't just leading a day trip to the canyon to admire its grandeur. He was leading an expedition into the unknown. At that time little was known about the land west of the Mississippi River. The uncharted land was filled with potential risks and rewards. Powell led with conviction and purpose, knowing he had to move forward by faith in order to confirm his hopes and dispel his fears.

We mention Powell because, as leaders in an American church, we believe his leadership speaks to the challenges the American church faces today. The future is unknown, but there is a general sense that the status quo is no longer working. Pastors are looking for new models, new structures, and new ways of being the church. Yet doing something new isn't simple or easy. It takes courage and faith.

The early days of the multisite revolution felt like a frontier expedition.[1] When the idea of a multisite church began gaining traction around the turn of the millennium, the multisite movement was the Old West meets the biblical days of the judges. Everyone was doing what was right in their own eyes on the frontier. Churches were isolated and breaking new ground. Very little was known about this new multisite phenomenon. And even less was known about the implications of adopting this new model because there were so few examples to learn from. Yet despite the risk inherent in trying something new and unknown, over the past two decades thousands of churches have ventured onto this uncharted path in increasing numbers.

Today, over 5 million people worship in one of the more than 8,000 multisite churches, making up 9 percent of American Protestant church-goers and 3 percent of American Protestant churches.[2] In the last quarter of a century, the multisite revolution has gone from an experiment to a widespread phenomenon. It has been adopted by all types of churches—denominationally, theologically, and geographically—and the trend shows no sign of slowing down.

Newton's Third Law states that for every action, there is an equal and opposite reaction. At the risk of stretching this illustration, we think the same has been true of the multisite phenomenon. For every church that has enthusiastically adopted and promoted the multisite church model as an anointed movement and a fresh work of God, there has been an equal and opposite response from other churches. Opponents of multisite castigate it, with some attributing its emergence to a work of Satan.[3]

Whether you are a fan or a critic of multisite, the multisite model isn't disappearing anytime soon. Noted evangelical researcher Ed Stetzer has predicted, "Multisite churches are on the rise. This is not a fad, this is not some sort of temporary trend—multisite churches are here to stay. It's like the megachurch now—just a part of our church landscape—the new normal."[4] Over the past fifteen years, the success of several high profile multisite churches has led to the model's exponential growth. As more churches adopt the model, it moves further into the mainstream of the evangelical church. In fact, the rapid growth of multisite has outpaced the megachurch movement by fivefold over a fifteen-year time span.[5] Additionally, multisite churches are led predominantly by young pastors with even younger congregations, adding to the intrigue of the movement. Is this a sign of fearless faith or the hubris of youth?

How should the church respond to this growing movement? How do we evaluate this new model in light of the Scriptures? Should we resist the multisite revolution or embrace it? And what are we to make of the well-meaning voices who question the validity and wisdom of the multisite model? These voices are asking many good and valid questions, like: Is this form of church biblical? Are we guilty of chasing after success rather than faithfully building up the body of Christ? What effect does multisite have on the spiritual growth and discipleship of people?

Many churches are adopting the multisite model because they want to faithfully fulfill the Great Commission and they see multisite as an opportunity to reach even more people for Jesus. Sadly, some of these same churches are embracing multisite without fully understanding the implications of their decision.

It is never easy to evaluate a movement in the early years of its development. Like the preseason rankings in college football, there are so many factors over the course of a season affecting the final standings that the wise course of action is delaying serious predictions until some of the dust has settled. There comes a point in the middle of the season when the picture becomes clearer. You are able to see what kind of team you have by evaluating past performance, and this helps project outcomes as you look ahead to the future.

We think the multisite movement has arrived at that place. Having reached a certain level of permanence and normality, it is now time to evaluate the churches, leaders, members, and ministries this movement has spawned.

To this end, we have designed our book to offer seasoned reflections on the multisite reality. We are asking: What have we learned? What has worked? What has not worked? And what might the future hold for this still-evolving movement? This book examines the multisite movement in light of the Scriptures, while articulating the lessons we have learned over the past fifteen or so years.

Our goal must go beyond a simple assessment of the past. We are leaders in a burgeoning church-planting network experimenting with a new church model as we continue to evolve. We call this new model *multichurch*. We believe the multichurch model is both a biblically grounded and a theologically sound ecclesiological model. Furthermore, multichurch provides a compelling solution to much of the rampant ecclesiological reductionism we find scattered across the contemporary American church.

Multichurch requires mature, humble, and expanding leadership, while fostering greater contextualization and ownership at the congregational level. A healthy multichurch results in a more active and engaged church that lives out its convictions in ways a single site church may not. Unlike multisite, multichurch is more than a church growth strategy. Multichurch encourages, with intentionality, the multigifted members of the church to develop into the vibrant, mature, and multiplying body God calls them to be.

So who is this book written for? The target audience is threefold. First, if you are a pastor, leader, or staff member of an existing multisite church, we hope this book will help you identify the multisite model you currently use and alert you to some of the key strengths, weaknesses, and challenges you are likely to face. Second, if you are a pastor, leader, or staff member of a single site church planning to become multisite, we believe our book will help you assess which multisite model would be best for your church. Additionally, we hope this new vision of multichurch provides a solution for some of the challenges ahead. Finally, if you are a member of one of the above churches and you want to better understand what a multisite church is and how it works, our book will introduce you to all of this and explain the multisite phenomenon. *MultiChurch* offers different models of churches, key principles, concrete examples, and helpful exercises for you to assess your church and plan for its future.

Both of us (Brad and Gregg) have extensive experience in leading multisite churches and, more recently, leading the new model, multichurch, introduced in this book. Brad worked at the upper levels of leadership at (the former) Mars Hill Church in Seattle, Washington, and currently serves as the executive pastor for churches and ministries at

Sojourn Community Church in Louisville, Kentucky.[6] Gregg has written a biblical and theological justification for multisite churches and serves as a nonstaff pastor on the leadership council of Sojourn.[7] Each of us has served as consultants with churches around the country that are exploring multisite solutions. We hope our collective experience will be helpful as we present what we have learned about multisite churches—what they are, how they work, what's worked and what hasn't, and how we can learn from our mistakes.

Let's be honest. John Wesley Powell muttered plenty of unrecorded comments during his expeditions that should not be quoted in this book. That's because charting new territory is full of setbacks, mistakes, and unexpected challenges that can cause frustration and, possibly, the occasional cursing. Romanticizing the pains of frontier life will not do anyone any good. Frontiers are distinguished by ambiguity, trial and error, and a distinct lack of resources. By sharing what we have learned, we hope to remedy some of these deficiencies and help you avoid some preventable setbacks. These lessons will include an introduction to an emerging model that we are excited about and believe to be the evolution of the multisite model: multichurch.

Defining the Terms

When you are heading to a new country, it is wise to learn as much as you can about the place you are visiting. This is especially true when you will be spending time away from urban areas, out in the countryside. As you prepare for a trip like this, you should familiarize yourself with the wildlife, plant life, terrain, and even local laws you might encounter. The saying "an ounce of prevention is worth a pound of cure" is particularly true when discovering whether the local mushrooms are edible or identifying if the public lands are legal to camp on.

Growing up in Michigan, I (Brad) spent a good deal of my young adult life camping and hiking. I was quite familiar with navigating the rules and etiquette of state parks and trails. A few months after moving to Seattle, I found myself on a last-minute camping trip with friends on the coast of the Olympic National Park. Confident in my previous experience, I did not bother with inconveniences like reading signs or posted park rules.

After a long day of hiking, it was getting late, and we stumbled on a perfect spot to camp and promptly fell asleep. I awoke early the next morning to a flashlight in my face. My confidence afforded me the opportunity to explain to a park ranger why I had pitched my tent in the middle of a wildlife preserve. Thankfully, it was not difficult to convince her of my ignorance, and I avoided a felony trespassing charge. This lesson has served me well as a pastor, teaching me to take the time to familiarize myself with the language, assumptions, and terms before I hike unwittingly into a new challenge.

In the same way, we begin our journey into multisite by learning the lay of the land. Therefore, we will get started by defining some of the key concepts and terms we will be using throughout this book. In simple terms, a *multichurch* is one church made up of multiple interdependent churches. We do not claim to have been the first to coin the term *multichurch*, but we are using it in a specific way, to mean something distinct from three other common terms: church, denomination (or network), and multisite.

Church can be defined in many ways. The Bible offers various images of the church as the people of God (1 Peter 2:9), the body of Christ (1 Cor. 12:27), and the temple of the Holy Spirit (1 Cor. 3:16–17). As "a pillar and foundation of the truth" (1 Tim. 3:15), the church professes and defends "the faith that was once for all entrusted to God's holy people" (Jude 3), including belief in the Trinity, the deity and humanity of Jesus Christ, the accomplishment of salvation by Christ's death and resurrection, the grace-filled application of such salvation through the Word and the Spirit of God, and more. Additionally, the ancient creeds described the church as "the communion of saints" possessing the attributes of oneness (or unity), holiness (progress in sanctification), catholicity (or universality of mission), and apostolicity (committed to the teachings of the apostles, or Scripture). At the time of the Reformation, the marks of the church were enumerated as rightly preaching and obediently hearing the Word of God, with the regular administration of baptism and the Lord's Supper.[8]

All of these elements help define the church. In its broadest sense, the church is a gospel-centered community characterized by preaching the Bible, celebrating baptism, and taking the Lord's Supper. According to the Lutheran *Augsburg Confession*, "The church is the congregation of the saints in which the gospel is rightly taught and the sacraments rightly administered. And unto the true unity of the church, it is sufficient to agree concerning the doctrine of the gospel and the administration of the sacraments."[9] This is the church united and defined at the broadest level.[10]

Beyond this basic biblical and theological definition of a church, many churches unite themselves with other churches to form a *denomination*. Churches in a denomination agree on certain theological, missional, and philosophical commonalities (like liturgy or an approach to ministry), and choose to relate together and distinguish themselves from other churches. Thus, we have Presbyterian, Methodist, Lutheran, Baptist, Pentecostal, Anglican churches, and many more. Denominations often share media outlets, educational institutions, missions agencies, training, and other resources. A *network* bears some resemblance to a denomination. In a network, churches also collaborate around shared doctrinal, missional, and philosophical commonalities, but *network* is often used in reference to groups of churches united around a specific purpose such as church planting, with less centralized authority than a denomination. Examples of networks include Acts 29, Redeemer City to City, Sojourn Network, ARC, Summit Network, Soma, and PLNTD.

Expressing unity more narrowly, *multisite* brings together a number of locations with several commonalities. The original definition given by Bird, Surratt, and Ligon in *The Multi-Site Church Revolution* explains: "A multisite church shares a common vision, budget, leadership, and board."[11] But this is the bare minimum. There is even more shared among the locations of a multisite church, including all the commonalities listed in our definition of church (gospel-centeredness, preaching and teaching the Word of God, celebrating baptism and the Lord's Supper) and the commonalities listed in our definition of denomination/network (doctrinal statement, mission focus, core values, and ministry philosophy). These common matters of faith, vision, practice, resources, leadership, and ministry unite a multisite church.

To be even more specific, a multisite church is any church that does not limit its gathering to one location and time. When a church broadcasts what is transpiring in its main auditorium to an overflow room, or when it adds a second (or third) service, it has taken the first steps into the realm of multisite. But this is only one type of multisite. Other multisite churches may have multiple venues, multiple sites, or different geographic locations. While this broad definition can be helpful, we will continue to clarify multisite in chapter 2 as we break down its specific expressions.[12]

One of those expressions has separated itself into its own category: *multichurch*. As we define it, multichurch is a local community of Christians that matures and multiplies its influence through launching, developing, and resourcing *multiple congregations to reach its city* with the gospel of Jesus Christ. This is one church with multiple congregations or "churches" in a set geographic area (bounded by an identifiable population that shares proximity and accessibility). Among the various congregations, a multichurch shares several key characteristics:

1. A multichurch shares all the characteristics of a single church: it is a gospel-centered community characterized by preaching the Bible and celebrating baptism and the Lord's Supper.
2. A multichurch shares all the broader commonalities of a denomination or network: it shares specific theological, missional, and philosophical commitments.
3. A multichurch has all the narrower commonalities inherent in multisite churches: it shares a common vision, mission, budget, strategy, resources, leadership, and ministry.

So what distinguishes a *multichurch* from a typical multisite church? A multichurch is one church expressed in multiple *churches*. These churches have a form of polity that provides the opportunity and authority to make decisions about budget, contextualization of ministries, and more. A multichurch engages in worship, perhaps with a common liturgy among the congregations and in multiple services across multiple locations in the city. A multichurch develops community, perhaps through groups such as missional communities or community groups, in which discipleship, care, and mission are carried out. A multichurch embarks on mission by communicating the gospel, living out the gospel together, and doing works of mercy on behalf of the poor, the homeless, the marginalized, and the suffering in its city. If this isn't entirely clear yet, don't worry! We will discuss this further in chapter 2.

What motivates the formation and fuels the development of a multichurch? There are several answers to this. A multichurch has a vision to spread God's fame throughout its city and believes this is best done through the empowerment of multiple leaders and congregations working together. It dreams about reaching the entire city with the gospel of Jesus Christ. A multichurch believes the gospel changes everything: individuals, marriages, families, neighborhoods, educational/social/economic/political structures, working conditions, and systemic sins like racism, sexism, and abortion. A multichurch fosters a climate where leaders do life and ministry together. It nurtures service where members are equipped to exercise their spiritual gifts and are challenged to develop as leaders. It insists on building up and living out community as the various congregations covenant together and collaborate to reach their city, in the broadest sense of that word "reach" (i.e., to expose the gospel, lead to Christ, disciple, teach, equip for maturity and multiplication, and launch on mission).

Again, to put it simply, a multichurch is a local community of maturing Christians who multiply their influence by launching, developing, and resourcing multiple congregations to reach its city with the gospel of Jesus Christ.

We are now familiar with the terrain and clear about the use of the terms *church*, *denomination*, *network*, *multisite*, and *multichurch*. Let's take a quick look at the map for our journey!

Reading the Trail Map

After this introduction and the overview of Sojourn's story in chapter 1, this book continues in three sections: "Scouting," "Orienteering," and "Setting Out." Section 1, "Scouting," will provide perspective by examining biblical, historical, and contemporary developments within the multisite movement. These initial four chapters will develop and demonstrate the biblical and theological soundness of multichurch.

Chapter 2, "Landscape," rehearses the story of the multisite movement, from its New Testament basis onward through contemporary developments. The chapter will detail biblical and theological foundations for multichurch, highlighting the work of the Holy Spirit.

Chapter 3, "Landmarks," sets forth seven different church models. These models are (1) pillar, (2) gallery, (3) franchise, (4) federation, (5) cooperative, (6) collective, and (7) network. Each of these models will be defined, explained in terms of their degree of unity/shared resources and leadership structure, and illustrated with examples. Additionally, we will offer an assessment of the strengths and weaknesses of each model with respect to the biblical and theological foundations we developed in the second chapter. By presenting the various models, we will show that some of the "generic" critiques of multisite churches have assumed homogeneity of multisite models. In reality, most of the criticisms are directed against a few models, and other models are not as susceptible to these challenges.

Chapter 4, "Landmines," puts the movement under the microscope and looks for the problems to avoid in adopting a multisite model. We want to take seriously the best criticisms and learn from the concerns raised about multisite methodology. Some of the charges are plausible and will inform the models we recommend. Other arguments against multisite don't hold up to scrutiny, yet they may still provide some value for evaluating the multichurch methodology in order to avoid drifting into dangerous directions that could lead to future failure.

Chapter 5, "The Future," lays out our vision for multichurch, what we see as an exciting new development on the multisite horizon. We will start with a biblical picture of the church and explore how the multichurch concept addresses many of the key concerns critics have with the multisite phenomenon and, in doing so, positively creates a thriving environment for members and leaders of the church.

The next five chapters form the second section of the book that we call "Orienteering" because it begins the process of mapping solutions and advantages in five key areas. Chapter 6, "MultiOrg," discusses the organization of multichurches. It offers three key maxims that drive multichurch, and their implications. Additionally, this chapter provides a few tools to help you evaluate your church and its organizational principles.

Chapter 7, "MultiPolity," addresses the matter of church government and the proper leadership structure required for a multichurch. Furthermore, it introduces the concept of redemptive polity and gives real-world examples of multichurch polity embracing these concepts.

Chapter 8, "MultiMinistry," tackles ministry in a multichurch context. It considers some of the unique challenges of ministry in this context and gives practical tools for establishing a conviction-driven philosophy of ministry. This chapter also illustrates how multichurch models can resist the tendency to move toward ecclesiological reductionism, while underscoring the important values required to develop a culture where ministry thrives.

Chapter 9, "MultiMoney," discusses financial matters in a multichurch structure. It explores four pernicious myths related to finances with the goal of helping those within, or considering, multichurch models to avoid the mistakes to which these myths lead.

Chapter 10, "MultiMembership," addresses members in a multichurch context. While people are members of the one church, they identify, through their attendance and service, with one specific congregation. As such, they are accorded many opportunities and advantages, which will be highlighted.

Section 3, "Setting Out," has the goal of preparing you and your church for a possible transition to a multichurch model. Chapter 11, "Navigating Transition," provides key principles for leading the transition into a multichurch model. This chapter outlines a basic transition plan and provides some lessons to make your transition as smooth as possible.

The book concludes with chapter 12, "The Rest of the Story," which completes the narrative of Sojourn's evolution into a multichurch. The purpose in sharing our story is to provide a real-world example of how our church was conceived, launched, and developed as one model, then re-conceived and re-launched, and has eventually evolved into other models, ending with the most recent transition to a multichurch model. Our goal in this chapter is to share the lessons learned (and mistakes made) throughout this process, to help those moving toward a multi-church expression, and to give an example for those in the middle of their own transition.

That's where we are heading. Now that we have the lay of the land and some basic definitions, let's get started!

A MultiChurch Evolution

The multisite movement has been and continues to be in a state of flux. Indeed, one of the characteristics of this movement is constant evolution. Such fluidity drives many people crazy—especially critics of multisite.

What is true of the multisite movement is also true of multisite churches: they evolve. Multisite leaders are fond of borrowing a phrase from startup companies that boast about "building the plane in the air." This is a necessary hazard of frontier development. Whether a church or a company, you chart new territory without the comfort of examples that have gone before you or the time required to test ideas before employing them. We are not beholden to some arbitrary clock of success, but learning through trial and error is often more time-efficient. Cutting-edge movements are driven by those willing to risk boldly rather than those who are bogged down with "paralysis by analysis."[1] This leads to more mistakes but also increases the chance of success. For those of us involved in building the plane, the messiness is exciting, frustrating, and very real—just part of our everyday experience!

As we begin this book, we trace for you the evolution of a particular multichurch: Sojourn Community Church. Every church story is unique in some sense, and while our story at Sojourn is irreproducible, it is helpful for other churches to get a concrete and real-world example of how a multichurch can develop. This is *not* a story of how we, with clear eyes and strong hearts, looked into the future and nimbly plotted a path to multichurch success. On the contrary, the more appropriate image is me walking through my living room in the dark, stepping on Legos, banging into the couch, stubbing my toe, suppressing a curse, and fumbling for the light switch. So with expectations clarified, let us share in brief how we got to where we are today.

The Mother of Invention

Sojourn was a church plant in January of 2000 that started like many church plants. About a dozen young Christians, full of angst and ideology in Louisville, Kentucky, began gathering and prayerfully seeking to reimagine what it means to be the church. Like most church plants, church structures beyond the traditional single-service model were not even on our radar. Borne of deep theological convictions, some overrealized preferences, and a dash of naiveté, a single-site church was planted to reach people in our context.

Within three years Sojourn had two hundred people attending. Many of these had been previously unchurched (turned off by religion and thus strangers to church) or overchurched (involved in traditional, often legalistic churches and thus burned out on formal Christianity). Sojourn had two emphases during this time: all members gathering for worship on Sunday (one church with one service) and then scattering throughout the week into community groups. In its third year, Sojourn became financially self-sustaining. At the heart of this growth was the conviction that the gospel changes everything—human hearts, interpersonal relationships, work, play, families, the city, and the world. Driven by these convictions and seeing a pattern of growth, Sojourn had little reason to think about other structures of church at that time.

Like most nomadic church plants, the congregation bounced around between leases until it found a little fixer-upper it could afford. Few things change your reality like home ownership. After I purchased my first house, many things changed. I found myself caring way too much about the length and quality of my lawn, not to mention the outrage I carried regarding this newly discovered offense known as "homeowner's dues." I knew the joys of having a place to entertain friends and the responsibilities of ownership.

Home ownership brings with it many changes that can be similar for church plants. Having a brick-and-mortar permanent location brings legitimacy to the church, which cannot be faked by a good social media presence. The city looks at you differently and so does your congregation. For us, having a permanent location ushered in a new season of growth and, with it, a few new problems.

One of those problems was, believe it or not, Sojourn's physical stability. Permanence meant that as we grew, we no longer had the option to lease a bigger space. We were what we were: constrained by the size of our auditorium space.

These constraints drove us to an early expression of multisite as we began multiple services to accommodate growth. Practically speaking, we had few options. Turning people away who wanted to hear the gospel was simply not an option. This move to a multisite expression was driven pragmatically by a need for space, and little thought was given to the trajectory on which this set the church. This pattern of growth is typical for most churches as they stumble into multisite.

During this time, multisite was becoming all the rage. A team of church members was commissioned to study the theological implications and biblical plausibility of this "new" methodology popping up around the country. Sojourn had a conviction to plant more churches in Louisville and at that point had already planted three. It was time to have a conversation about integrating this new idea.

Gregg was commissioned to lead the theological study. The group read *The Multi-Site Church Revolution: Being One Church . . . in Many Locations* (Zondervan, 2006). At the time, this was the only book-length treatment of this movement. They also read various articles on the phenomenon and interviewed several churches (Highview Baptist in Louisville, Bethlehem Baptist Church in Minneapolis, and Harbor Presbyterian Church in San Diego). In the end, the idea was mothballed until our multiple service solution to growth reached its limits.

As the old proverb states, "Necessity is the mother of invention." Like most forays into multisite beyond multiple services, we took our first steps toward multisite because we ran out of options. We could not keep up with growth, so we needed another solution. We would have preferred to have chosen multisite out of conviction, but in reality multisite chose us.

Eyes Larger Than Our Stomach

Despite the research done during our "multiservice" phase, Sojourn had precious little to go on when we decided to become a multisite church. To reinforce the idea that multisite chose us, you could describe the next phase of our existence as "the season of opportunism." This too is typical for churches as they enter into multisite. Rather than being proactive, prayerfully and deliberately planting a new location, many multisite churches are reactive, responding to opportunities that come their way. We were no different. While looking for a solution to significant growth and considering the possibility of multisite, another local church offered to partner with Sojourn. Fifty members from Sojourn joined with this small group, and our second site officially launched. This transition was fairly smooth, which was a testament to Sojourn's leadership. However, this is not always the case. We're sure it is difficult to imagine two merging churches having any problems, but trust us, smooth transitions are worth rejoicing over.

Although this new experiment was fueled by several pragmatic considerations, we also kept in mind the biblical values that surfaced through our earlier investigation of multisite. Could the biblical virtues of interdependence, connectedness, cooperation, and unity—expressed in the motto "life and ministry together"—be realized through this new model of multisite?

One of the first hurdles we faced was how to unify the preaching of two campuses. Our solution was to have Daniel Montgomery, one of the founding pastors of Sojourn, drive between locations and preach at all the services. Many ventures into multisite start this way. That might be due, in part, to the exotic idea of riding the circuit with your Bible in the wind like old John Wesley himself. Unfortunately, like most fantasies, the reality is quite different. The challenge of coordinating multiple services and the toll it took on the preacher made this solution unsustainable, which prompted us to change course and hire a full-time pastor for our second campus. As you can see, it didn't take long before we had to start improvising.

During the next two years we became addicted to improvisation. While the second campus was still establishing itself, new opportunities came our way. Even though our first location was being held together by a bare-bones staff and some amazing volunteers, we pursued some of these new opportunities. Another church gifted us a building and merged its dwindling congregation into Sojourn. As if we weren't changing enough, we purchased a building across the river in southern Indiana to start our third location within three years. Sojourn rapidly expanded to be a church of four campuses in the greater Kentuckiana region.

If this sounds chaotic, that's because it was. We had not developed a clear plan for moving to a multisite model, so most of the decisions we made were in reaction to growth and the other challenges the church faced. At the time, we had few resources to lean on. This "reactive" leadership put a significant amount of strain on the staff and volunteers as the church expanded.

All of this was extremely exciting, as growth always is. However, our eyes were bigger than our stomach. As we will discuss in future chapters, multisite has the unfortunate advantage of helping churches to expand faster than the leadership can grow to lead them.

Sojourn had embraced the vision of "one church in several locations," but knew little of the implications of this model. In those first three years, things were moving so fast that we had little time to worry about it. But as the dust settled, we began to feel the pains of rapid growth and organizational ambiguity. We burned out several good leaders who were instrumental in our success. Because we weren't sure what multisite would look like in the future, we hired leaders with job descriptions that quickly became obsolete. All the things that made the growth phase so exciting started to lose their luster. People got tired of reorganizations, reinventions, re-visioning, and the like. We had grown to about 3,500 members, yet we had the infrastructure of a church of 800.

From Crisis to Change

Milton Friedman understood the mechanics of change. "Only a crisis— actual or perceived—produces real change. When that crisis occurs, the actions that are taken depend on the ideas that are lying around. That, I believe, is our basic function: to develop alternatives to existing policies, to keep them alive and available until the . . . impossible becomes the . . . inevitable."[2] This statement sums up the condition of Sojourn in the fall of 2012.

The crisis for us was the realization that our jerry-rigged multisite solution would not be sustainable long-term. Sojourn's leadership was autocratic, leaving our campus pastors feeling disconnected from decisions implemented at their campuses. As we will discuss in chapters 8 and 9, our ministry organization and finances placed a heavy burden on our campuses as they strained to maintain what we would later admit to be a bloated central staff.

Sojourn was unified on the vision of what we wanted to accomplish for the kingdom of Christ. But it was becoming increasingly clear that we needed to change our approach. We were staring in the face of Friedman's crisis.

The next season at Sojourn could be described as a soul-searching journey to redefine who and what we were as a church. We had many questions that needed to be answered. What did it mean to be a multisite church? How could we build a sustainable model? How did this affect our polity, ministries, and finances? These questions and more needed to be addressed, and it led to a complete reimagining of our church. You could say we needed to grow up as an organization in order to reflect the reality of our growth. Growing up required a change of polity, financial model, ministry model, and leadership structure.

The rest of this book is a look into our journey of discovery and reimagining of what it means to be a multisite church. Along the way we discovered a new vision of hope for building a church of multiple interdependent churches that through collaboration and unity can accomplish much more together for the kingdom of God. We call this vision multichurch. We believe it's the future of multisite.

The transition to a multichurch was much like the expeditions led by John Wesley Powell during the emergence of United States. A successful expedition required preparation, faith, and a little luck. In the following chapters we can help you with the first of these. As Powell said, "We may conjecture many things," but conjecture will not get us to our destination. We must begin the journey, so let's do some scouting.

SECTION 1

SCOUTING

While on top of Everest, I looked across the valley towards
the great peak Makalu and mentally worked out a route about
how it could be climbed. It showed me that even though I was
standing on top of the world, it wasn't the end of everything.
I was still looking beyond to other interesting challenges.

SIR EDMUND HILLARY

Scouting involves engaging in reconnaissance to prepare for an expedition.
The goal of scouting is to obtain information about the meteorological,
hydrographic, and geographic characteristics of a particular area.[1] You
would be foolish to attempt an expedition without first taking the time to
prepare and getting familiar with the potential dangers and opportunities
that lie ahead.

You may already be on the multisite journey—or perhaps you are just
getting started. As we look to the future, we believe the best place to start
is with a little scouting. What is the terrain, and where are the existing
paths and the dangerous places to avoid? Our goal in this section is to
find a high bluff, where we can look back at where we have come from
and discern the potential obstacles ahead. From here, we will be able to
see our destination on the horizon. Let's climb to the top and take a look.

Landscape

Multichurch—and the broader multisite movement for that matter—is nothing new. While it may seem like a recent phenomenon—something fresh, unique, and unprecedented—it's actually the latest variation on a very old way of doing church. Every generation is prone to what C. S. Lewis referred to as "chronological snobbery," the assumption that our time and our contributions are uniquely the best or the most advanced. The real story of multichurch, the idea of one church meeting as multiple congregations in a city, can be traced back to the first century, to the beginning of Christianity. It would be more accurate to say that contemporary manifestations are more of a renewal of early church methodology than a truly new development.

Multisite in the Early Church

The very first Christian church was a multisite church. The descent of the Holy Spirit on the morning of the day of Pentecost filled the 120 disciples and multitudes of onlookers with wonder (Acts 2:1–21). In response to Peter's preaching of the gospel (2:22–40), the initial group of Jesus's followers who had been baptized by the Spirit expanded, growing to about three thousand believers (2:41). This new, Spirit-generated church in Jerusalem was characterized by a number of elements. We read about them in Acts 2:42–45:

> They devoted themselves to the apostles' teaching and to fellowship, to the breaking of bread and to prayer. Everyone was filled with awe

at the many wonders and signs performed by the apostles. All the believers were together and had everything in common. They sold property and possessions to give to anyone who had need.

The apostles preached the gospel and explained how repentance and faith unites people to Jesus Christ. Identification with the death, burial, and resurrection of Christ, vividly portrayed through baptism, brought about the forgiveness of sins and the gift of the Holy Spirit (2:38). The new brothers and sisters in Christ experienced a deep sense of unity, flourishing in community and engaging in sacrificial giving. These new believers worshiped God "in spirit and truth" (John 4:24 ESV). They were true worshipers through the crucifixion—the broken body and shed blood—of Christ, clearly illustrated in the celebration of the Lord's Supper. These new disciples devoted themselves to prayer, praising and thanking God, rejoicing in their salvation, interceding for one another, and entreating God to rescue their family and friends through the gospel. And these new members witnessed God's confirmation of the gospel message and its messengers, as the apostles healed the sick, restored sight to the blind, exorcised demons, and raised the dead.

Where and when did all this activity take place? In two locations: in the temple and from house to house. And it all happened, we are told, on a daily basis (Acts 2:46).[1] The church in Jerusalem met day-to-day in a central location and in the disciples' homes. In the large gathering place of the temple, the apostles preached and performed signs and wonders, and the believers enjoyed fellowship, gave sacrificially, worshiped, and prayed. Likewise, in the smaller gatherings in homes, the apostles taught and did miracles, and the disciples lived in community, helped other disciples and the poor, worshiped, and prayed. This dual-structured gathering occurred regularly: "Day after day, in the temple courts and from house to house, they never stopped teaching and proclaiming the good news that Jesus is the Messiah" (Acts 5:42). One such expression of the church of Jerusalem was the group that met in the house of Mary (Acts 12:12). The Bible tells us that the church of Jerusalem gathered together in the temple, *and* the church of Jerusalem gathered together in homes.[2]

And what we find in Jerusalem was true in other cities as well. The church in Rome met in various locations, and Paul sent greetings to the church that specifically gathered in the house of Priscilla and Aquila (Rom. 16:5).[3] The Roman church may have also consisted of Asyncritus, Phlegon, Hermes, Patrobas, Hermas, and other Christians meeting with them in a second house, as well as Philologus, Julia, Nereus and his sister, Olympas, and other Christians gathering with them in a third (Rom. 16:14–15). Similarly, the church of the Laodiceans assembled in various places, and Paul offered greetings to the specific congregation meeting in the house of Nympha (Col. 4:15).[4] If we engage in a bit of informed speculation, we can imagine the Corinthian Christians gathering as "the whole church," perhaps in the house of Gaius (Rom. 16:23; 1 Cor. 14:23), and as the church assembled in the house of Titius Justus (Acts 18:7), the home of Crispus (Acts 18:8), and the house of Stephanas (1 Cor. 16:15). Whether meeting all together as the whole church in a large house or space, or congregating as parts of the church in smaller homes, the assemblies were considered to be *the church*: one church existing as multiple congregations or locations.[5]

Historical Development of Multisite

The multichurch structure in some form or another continued to characterize churches after the apostolic age. The one-bishop framework, initiated in the second century, developed into the early church's organization of a regional bishop leading all the churches in a geographical area. These provincial churches were part of one church under the bishop's authority, even though they existed as separate, geographic congregations. More to the point, the early church self-identified as "one, holy, catholic, and apostolic" (Nicene-Constantinopolitan Creed). The church was defined, not as many separate churches, but as one church. Developing from this identification today is the Roman Catholic Church, which still considers itself to be the one universal church with all local/geographic churches (or parishes) under its authority.

With the Protestant Reformation, however, new churches formed that did not recognize the authority of Rome. Presbyterian, Lutheran, and Anglican denominations incorporated strong elements that led to theological and structural bonds between their churches, distinct from the ecclesial authority of Rome. Protestant churches facing the fierce backlash of the Roman Catholic Church necessarily met in small enclaves, yet they felt unified and bound together as persecuted churches. As the persecution waned, many churches assembled in rural areas and hamlets, so their independence and unity owed more to demographic realities than anything else. Still, some associations were formed to provide connectedness for these churches.

As the church crossed the Atlantic, imbibing the spirit of American autonomy and democracy, many churches became characterized by a spirit of intense independence. For cultural reasons, the notion of the autonomous, independent church dominated the ecclesiastical scene. The unity of the church, so important in the New Testament and the early church, took a back seat for several hundred years in American Christianity. Over time, many churches recognized the deficiency and saw the need for a renewal of church collaboration.

Recovering Interdependence

The contemporary multisite phenomenon grew in fits and starts. A few attempts at expanding churches were made in the 1970s and 80s. For example, under the pastorate of Tim LaHaye, Scott Memorial Baptist Church in San Diego existed as two distinct geographic sites: Scott East and Scott West.[6] The 1980s saw a few more churches adopt a similar approach. In 1985, Northern Heights Lutheran Church in Minneapolis expanded to two locations. In 1987, Mount Paran Church of God in Atlanta transformed the facilities of the former Marietta Baptist Church into its second location, Mount Paran North.[7] Also in 1987, Jack Hayford's The Church on the Way in Van Nuys, California, turned the former First Baptist Church of that city into its west campus.[8]

While many churches in the United States experimented with multisite during these years, one church in particular is often considered by many church growth experts to be the pioneer of the multisite church movement in the 1980s. In the words of its founder, "I was the pastor of one of the first multiple-campus churches in America. We came to Atlanta with the plan to have 'one church, many congregations' in order to impact Atlanta. Within ten years we had four congregations spread over North Atlanta."[9] The year was 1989, and the pastor was Randy Pope, founder of Perimeter Church.

Pope planted the church with a four-part vision. First, he envisioned Perimeter Church as "one local congregation" with one hundred locations around Atlanta. Second, Perimeter Church would "have one senior pastor with local pastors at each congregation." Third, the leadership structure of Perimeter Church would have "one board with three representatives from 'each congregation.'" And finally, in terms of its mission Perimeter Church would have "one overall program of outreach conducted through each specific congregation."[10] Pope planted Perimeter in 1977. The second congregation, Perimeter West, was launched in Marietta in 1980. By 1990, Perimeter Church had four congregations.

Brian Frye gives several reasons why Perimeter Church rightly holds the distinction of being the first contemporary multisite church:

> First, Perimeter Church came into being with the explicit purpose of being one church in multiple locations. Other early multi-site type churches evolved or fell into the multi-site arrangement. . . . Second, Perimeter Church set a new precedent by moving beyond just a second site to a third and then a fourth site of a single church. While they would not achieve the 100 churches Pope envisioned, the church centered on a multi-site growth philosophy. Third, Perimeter Church inaugurated a novel church construct when it created a church in which both campuses (along with other campuses as they were launched) were interdependent and "co-autonomous" as one church functioning with the same leadership, nature, and purpose.[11]

While Perimeter Church was a forerunner, soon afterward several more churches considered the model and experimented with multisite.[12] Indeed, the 1990s witnessed the addition of several hundred additional multisite churches.[13] In 2003, the best count was that there were around one thousand multisite churches in the United States, and two years later that number had grown to about 1,500 churches.[14] By 2007, there were 2,000 multisite churches, and for the next two years an additional 500 churches were added each year: 2,500 in 2008 and 3,000 in 2009. Anticipating some of this growth, the first book on the movement was published in 2006—*The Multi-Site Church Revolution*—followed in 2009 by a sequel, *The Multi-Site Church Road Trip*.[15] Over the next five years the growth continued at an even more rapid pace. By early 2014, there were more than 8,000 multisite churches, with the number of worshipers attending multisite churches in excess of 5 million people.[16]

The rapid, quarter-century development of the multisite movement prompted Ed Stetzer to declare that multisite was here to stay, "not some sort of temporary trend" but "a part of our church landscape—the new normal."[17] While many pastors have been hearing about the megachurch trend (churches with more than 2,000 people in attendance at worship services), the reality is that the multisite movement has seen far greater growth over the past two decades. Today, there are far more multisite churches than megachurches (around 1,500 as of this writing). And a church does not have to be a megachurch to become a multisite church: the most common size of a multisite church is 1,300 people meeting in multiple locations on a given Sunday. Also, multisite churches have an unusually high success rate among new church plants—90 percent. They are not only effectively launching new congregations, but they are also planting other churches.[18]

The Primary Challenge to Multisite

Despite the growth and success of the multisite movement, it has not been without its share of criticism. In chapter 3, we will examine these in detail, but before we conclude this chapter we want to alert you to the key objection that most critics have with the model: the biblical and theological support, or the lack thereof, for doing it. In other words, while multisite might be effective and pragmatic, many pastors wonder: Is it biblical? Is multisite really a valid expression of church or is it a human innovation that destroys the integrity of what God has made? To answer this question, we will look at some positions that people take in favor of multisite, and consider some reasons why others urge *not* to use this model.

The Pragmatist: "Yes!" Because Multisite Works

Some hold the position that multisite is a legitimate expression of the church, but it needs no biblical and theological warrant. We offer three examples of this view. The first example can be called *menefreghismo*, a beautiful Italian word meaning "I couldn't care less." Those who take this position have no interest in providing any warrant for multisite, because they don't believe it is necessary. This is a wholly pragmatic position: whatever works is valid. Since multisite works to attract new, usually unreached people, it is good and right. Multisite expands the influence and reach of successful churches. The local church seems more accessible to people by providing them with something they recognize culturally. This is especially true of the "franchise" model. People are already accustomed to franchises such as McDonald's, Chick-fil-A, Chipotle, Target, Lowe's, Staples, and more. Inherent in this thinking is that like a franchise, a church provides goods and services. People expect churches to offer franchises close to where they live and work. Thus, multisite meets these cultural expectations and appeals to people today. Finally, if you doubt the validity of multisite, just look at the results! How can over 8,000 growing churches be wrong?

Other versions of this first position are slightly more sophisticated and thoughtful. Some proponents of multisite invoke *the normative principle*, which states that the church is free to incorporate any and all elements in its worship (e.g., guitars, robes for the ministers) unless Scripture either explicitly or implicitly prohibits them. Because Scripture does not explicitly or implicitly prohibit multisite, churches are free to structure themselves in this manner. As another example, some proponents appeal to the concept of *adiaphora*. Adiaphora are neither moral matters like loving one's neighbor, nor immoral matters like murder. Rather, they are indifferent matters before God. These are things we can choose to participate in and have his approval, or we can abstain from engaging in them and still have his approval. Biblical examples include eating meat sacrificed to idols and honoring one day above another (Romans 14; 1 Corinthians 8). Contemporary examples include preferring organic foods, schooling choices (public, private, Christian, or home school), and whether and how to celebrate Christmas and Easter. Because multisite is one of these *indifferent* matters, churches are free to structure themselves in this manner, and to do so with God's approval.

A final example of this first position claims that Scripture presents no prescriptive or normative pattern for structuring the church. Some will point out that churches with episcopalian, presbyterian, and congregational church governments all appeal to the same biblical texts in support of their system. To many, this lack of clarity points to the fact that Scripture itself does not set forth one type of church structure. Without any normative pattern laid down in Scripture, churches are free to structure themselves as they see fit to accomplish their mission, and multisite is a valid way of doing this.

The Naysayer: Saying "No!" to Multisite

On the opposite end is the position some take that multisite is illegitimate because it has no clear biblical or theological warrant. Again, there are various approaches that fall under this position. Some opponents of multisite invoke *the regulative principle* which "teaches that with regard to worship whatever is commanded in Scripture is required, and that whatever is not commanded is forbidden."[19] This is similar to those who see multisite as a matter of indifference (*adiaphora*) except that in this case one arrives at the opposite conclusion. Because Scripture does not explicitly or implicitly command multisite, churches are forbidden to structure themselves in this manner. As we have seen, however, there is biblical precedent for a church (for example, the church in Jerusalem, the church in Rome) to be a church in which its members gather in various houses rather than all together. So this argument is, at face value, difficult to sustain. A biblical pattern would, at the very least, allow a church to structure itself in a multisite manner, with the various sites or congregations corresponding to the various houses in which these early churches met.

Some go even further, objecting to multisite because the structure is contradictory to the biblical idea of the church.[20] Appeal is often made to the New Testament Greek word ἐκκλησία (*ekklēsia*), which means *assembly* or *gathering*: "On one level the question [of the biblical warrant for multisite churches] is settled lexically by simply considering the meaning of the word *ekklēsia*. The New Testament authors regularly use the word to mean 'assembly.' . . . [Churches assembling together is] essential to their identity as a group."[21] The conclusion of those opposed to the multisite model is that all church members *must necessarily* assemble together at the same time in the same location: "While a single congregation may meet *more* than once a week (e.g., by gathering a second time on Sunday evening or for a midweek meeting), it's difficult to see how they could do anything *less*."[22] Given in support of this idea are biblical examples of believers assembling together (Acts 20:7; 1 Cor. 16:2; Rev. 1:10; cf. Acts 2:46) and historical examples of church services from the second century.[23] Practical reasons for gathering together as one group are also provided. These include hearing God's Word read and preached, witnessing faith professed in baptism, taking the Lord's Supper, praying and singing together, teaching and giving, encouraging one another, and bearing one another's burdens and sorrows.[24]

Supporters of multisite agree with the reasons given. Certainly, Christians are to assemble together. In the New Testament this gathering is referred to with the word *ekklēsia*. However, *assembly* and *gathering* are not the only translations of this word. It can refer to meetings of Christians in particular houses (Acts 12:12), the church in a city (1 Cor. 1:1–2; 1 Thess. 1:1), all the churches in a region (Acts 9:31), the universal church (Matt. 16:18; Eph. 1:21–23), the Christian people (1 Cor. 10:32), and even the saints already in heaven (Heb. 12:23). Even when the word clearly means "assembly," *ekklēsia* itself does not indicate the manner of the assembly, that is, if it is a gathering of a few members, some members, many members, or all the members. Critics of multisite assume it is an assembly of *all* the church's members at the same time. But if this assumption is true, why does Paul specifically refer on two occasions to "the whole church" gathering together (Rom. 16:23; 1 Cor. 14:23)?[25] The word "whole" would be redundant if *ekklēsia* always means an assembly of *all* the church's members. Paul's use of the expression "the whole church" clearly implies the existence of an assembly in which *not all* the church's members are meeting.[26]

As we have shown in our earlier discussion of Acts 2:42–46 (as well as Acts 5:42), this is historically incorrect as well. The church of Jerusalem gathered together in the temple (an assembly of possibly all the members), and the church of Jerusalem gathered together in homes (an assembly of some, but clearly not all, of the members). Further illustrations include the church in Rome meeting in the house of Priscilla and Aquila (Rom. 16:5) and the church of the Laodiceans meeting in the house of Nympha (Col. 4:15). Only some of the members gathered in these houses, yet each of these smaller assemblies is still an *ekklēsia*—a church. Concluding that the multisite church model is unbiblical because it is not an assembly of *all* the members of the church is based on a faulty, assumed premise.

Furthermore, this critique commits the methodological error of defining a concept (*church*) by defining a word (*ekklēsia*). Developing our understanding of something as complex and glorious as the church on the definition of one word is precarious and misguided. We would never do this when discussing salvation (*sōteria*) or justification (*dikaiosunē*), concepts that are far richer in meaning than the mere definitions of the New Testament words. The same is true for our understanding of *church*; its meaning is much more than the definition of the word *ekklēsia*.

Moreover, this approach seems to overlook the New Testament's rich presentation of the church. The church was originally called "the Way" (Acts 9:2; 19:9, 23; 22:4; 24:14, 22), underscoring its association with Jesus, who himself is "the way" (John 14:6). Biblical metaphors for the church include the people of God, the body of Christ, and the temple of the Holy Spirit. Additionally, we have the rich historical development of the doctrine of the church handed down to us from the past. The church has been defined as "one, holy, catholic, and apostolic" (Nicene-Constantinopolitan

Creed), "the communion of saints" (Apostles' Creed), and the entity "in whom is the fixed number of the saints predestined before the foundation of the world" (Augustine).[27] Both the Scriptural presentation of the church, and the historical development of the doctrine of the church, indicate that we should avoid the methodological error of trying to define the *church* by defining the word (*ekklēsia*).

Why spend time on this criticism? Those who advance it end up dismissing thousands of vibrant churches that are actively advancing the kingdom of God. In a conversation we had with a young pastor who was steeped in this position, he lamented that it was a shame there are no "healthy churches" in China. His narrow ecclesiological understanding had led him to dismiss and devalue a tremendous movement of the Spirit within our generation. We should not constrain the work of God by forcing our personal preferences onto his church.

The Pioneer: "Yes!" Multisite is Biblical and Good

The third position, and the one we advocate, is neither the pragmatist nor the naysayer. We should not simply adopt a model because it works or because the Bible (allegedly) isn't clear about it. Nor should we limit what the Bible teaches by narrowing our understanding of the church to a simple definition. We believe that multichurch is legitimate *and* has biblical and theological warrant. We have already set forth some of the biblical precedent by looking at the church in Jerusalem, the very first Christian church, and how it existed as a multisite church. So, too, we've looked at the church in Rome, the church in Laodicea, and the church in Corinth, with additional locations possible. There is clear biblical precedent that the early Christian churches existed as one church meeting in multiple locations.

The multisite position has a solid theological justification as well.[28] One such warrant focuses on the theology of evangelism and mission: multisite promotes neighborhood missions. These churches, grasping the missional identity of the church, are designed with the specific missional purpose to reach their city with the gospel as a community. In a sense, multisite missions reverses the trend that takes people out of their neighborhood/relational networks in order to attend the church twenty-five minutes away from their home. Rather, it establishes congregations in multiple locations so as to affect all the neighborhoods in the city. Such multiplication promotes contextualization of the gospel to engage meaningfully with people and groups throughout the city that are quite different from one another.

Another justification focuses on discipleship and expansion: multisite is a way to incorporate significant growth from God. Such growth is a blessing, not a curse. A church that is experiencing God-given growth must expand and restructure in order to accommodate the growth and minister effectively. For example, during the pastorate of John Piper, Bethlehem Baptist Church, because of its rapid growth, opted "for 'spreading' by multiplication as opposed to the more comfortable mindset of expansion by centralized enlargement." Thus, its vision for extension encompassed the multiplication of "churches and campuses," that is, the creation and development of a multisite church in the Minneapolis/St. Paul area and church planting elsewhere, but not (physical) expansion of its downtown Minneapolis location.[29] This multisite approach allowed Bethlehem Baptist Church to fulfill its biblical obligation to disciple the many people who came to Christ, in part, through its ministry.

It should be noted that we are not equating numeric growth with spiritual health. Not all healthy churches experience the kind of growth that requires such restructuring. However, in the cases where the Spirit does bring significant growth, a multichurch solution can accommodate this blessing and help the church care for its members.

The criticism that the solution to such sizeable growth is church planting overlooks an important reality: it is easy to talk about church planting but very difficult to do. Even if another church is planted in the city, it is difficult to send away part of the congregation to that daughter church, especially if it is a significant distance away from the mother church. Thus, that church plant cannot effectively relieve the pressure of the growth of the mother church. Additionally, a new church plant that is still relatively immature is often incapable of attracting and handling growth from the mother church.

As for additional justification, studies have shown that multisite is an effective approach for (1) "reaching more people" with the gospel, (2) "stewarding resources" (multiplying locations or congregations costs less than church planting), and (3) "multiplying ministries and leadership."[30] Additionally, as the example of Bethlehem Baptist demonstrates, churches do not have to choose between multiplying congregations and planting churches: they can do both.[31] The track record of Sojourn Community Church reflects this truth as well. From the beginning of Sojourn the leadership team, led by Daniel Montgomery, was committed to church planting. To this end, over the past sixteen years four churches were planted in the same geographic area, twelve were planted outside our geographic area, and three multisite locations were planted. Only two of the locally planted churches still exist, and they are reaching about 300 people in total. The external church plants have fared much better, reaching roughly 4,000 people altogether. The multisite congregations have grown to reach approximately 2,500 more people than when they were planted. Our experience confirms the findings that this methodology is an effective approach to expanding the kingdom of God.

Another warrant focuses on the virtues that multisite nourishes: multisite fosters the biblical and theological values of unity, cooperation, and interdependence. Because of the commonalities shared among their locations, multisite churches embody these biblical virtues in concrete ways. Pastors engage regularly, often weekly or even daily, in deep relationships, prayer, mutual accountability, preparation of sermons, pastoral care, crisis management, and more. This point does not deny that such values can be nurtured in structures other than multisite. They certainly can be. Multisite, however, is an intentional arrangement whereby these virtues flourish.

Conclusion

This chapter has laid out the historical development of multisite and provided a biblical and theological foundation for the structure. Yet multisite is not without its detractors. Several concerns challenge this methodology, and as we prepare to address these concerns, we must recognize that a fair amount of confusion and generalization regarding multisite churches exists. With this in mind, we believe the starting point for evaluating these concerns is to clearly present the various models of multisite. This enables us to more accurately evaluate concerns by looking at the different expressions of the movement individually, which will be the focus of the next chapter.

3

Landmarks

In chapter 2, we laid out a historical and biblical foundation for multisite as an acceptable church model. We also responded to the movement's primary challenge: its alleged lack of biblical and theological support. However, we stopped short of addressing any other common concerns because of the complexity and diversity among multisite models. Simply put, not all multisite churches are the same. This chapter will discuss seven church models, five of which form a spectrum of multisite expressions. Within this spectrum we locate multichurch. The diversity among multisite models reflects the church's creative impulses to advance the kingdom of God and proclaim the gospel. Therefore, before we discuss each model in detail, we will begin by exploring the implications of God's creativity and how examining divine creativity might better prepare us to evaluate the models.

The Creative Impulse

God is creative. He is first introduced to us in the Bible as the Creator, the maker of all things. What he made exudes creativity in its beauty, diversity, splendor, elegance, and fruitfulness. Although we might refer to him as Creator in song or prayer, we rarely spend time thinking about the significance of his creativity for who we are as the church. We are a gathered collection of God's image-bearers, but at times those God-given creative impulses are suppressed within the church. Even when we do embrace them, they are almost exclusively reflected in the context of visual or performing arts.

Creativity, however, is more than the visual arts. It is a divine attribute that God shares with his image-bearers, and it flows through *every* aspect of our lives. We are by nature creative beings, and this trait applies to problem solving as much as it does to painting a landscape, and to our ministry systems as much as it does to writing worship songs. Why do we raise this point? Because we believe it honors God when we give our attention to the beauty expressed in composing an elegant church structure. We should be able to cultivate and appreciate beauty in the organizational structure of a church, much like we are able to see the divine glory and transcendence in the architecture of a majestic medieval church building.

This is more than just an exercise in aesthetics. By acknowledging beauty, we are reminded of the importance of divinely given creativity in the development of our organization models. By emphasizing creativity, we hope it will lead more people on church leadership teams to turn to Scripture and prayer—rather than business journals and analytics—as they contemplate organizational changes. An appreciation of beauty and creativity can diffuse our defensiveness toward new expressions of the church, as we can sometimes be guilty of protecting our preferences. When we see the creative character of God in the innovative impulse to advance his kingdom, we become encouragers and counselors rather than critics. When church leaders are gripped with fear, they compulsively try to tear others down. Instead, by regarding the creativity of others as imaging our creative God, we are free to appreciate, evaluate, and even learn from different models.

When the church is unwilling to embrace the creative impulse, it loses opportunities to advance the gospel. Many opportunities have been missed in the name of doing things as they have always been done. As Henry Ford reminds us, "If I had asked people what they wanted, they would have said a faster horse." On the contrary, Paul brags that he has "become all things to all people" (1 Cor. 9:22) that he might bring some to salvation. Paul was willing to innovate to reach more people for Jesus.

Chairman Mao's attempt to purge China of Christians and their influence propelled the church to be innovative as well. In China, when Pastor Chang was arrested—not once, not twice, but three times—he gathered with other believers in the prison for mutual support and Bible study. They encouraged one another to share the gospel among the nonbelieving prisoners. As the number of the disciples grew, small churches were planted in different parts of the prison. This church-planting movement within Chinese prisons grew exponentially. When these believers were eventually set free, they returned home to plant new house churches that formed the backbone of the underground church that propelled the kingdom of God throughout China. In the face of persecution, creative innovation resulted not only in new churches but also in a movement that changed China's religious landscape forever.[1]

This is not to say that the outcome of our creativity is ever flawless—or even always acceptable. If you have ever painted, written a song or a book, or otherwise tried to create something, you understand the difference between the creative impulse and the outcome. They don't always match up. When we think about the organizational structures of the church, our creative inspiration can be drawn from many places. Sometimes the outcome is an elegant solution to advance the kingdom. Sometimes the result is a hodgepodge that creates more of a headache than it alleviates. But this is the reality of thinking creatively.

We purposefully began with a few words on creative thinking before we examined the seven models of multisite churches. We want to encourage you to evaluate the various models and, rather than beginning with the flaws of each model, to begin by appreciating the God-given creative impulse that fuels each of these approaches. Then you can better evaluate each of these solutions to church growth and commitment to mission based on their ability to reveal truth about the creative character of God.

The Spectrum

So what are the seven models? These expressions represent a range of church structures. We have chosen to delineate them across a spectrum based on what we call the *locus of power*. The locus of power is the authority and the responsibility to establish vision, make decisions, and spend money. Across the spectrum, the locus of power moves from complete centralization on the left to strong decentralization on the right.

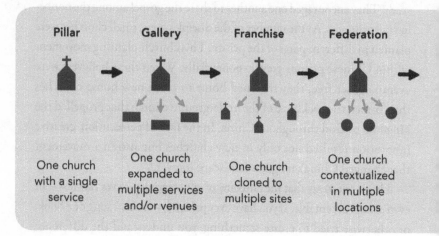

Pillar	Gallery	Franchise	Federation
One church with a single service	One church expanded to multiple services and/or venues	One church cloned to multiple sites	One church contextualized in multiple locations

As we evaluated the growth and development of the multisite movement, we identified seven models, which are (1) pillar, (2) gallery, (3) franchise, (4) federation, (5) cooperative, (6) collective, and (7) network. More precisely, the five models in the middle (from gallery to collective) represent the various models of multisite. We identified distinctions related to the locus of power in each structure.

As we begin looking at the different models, we want to point out that there has been some debate over the past several years about how to refer to the various sites of a multisite church. Some favor the terms *campuses* or *congregations*, while others argue that they should be called *churches*, which fuels the debate on what constitutes a church. While a church is characterized by many elements (worship, discipleship, mercy, and mission), key for our discussion is the fact that a church has a distinct form of government.

Some have taken this to mean that a site without its own pastor(s) is a *campus* while a site with its own pastor(s) can more properly be called a *church*. Although this line of argument has some merit, we believe it is insufficient because it does not address the ability of those pastors to actually engage in the governance of their church. It is one thing to be called a pastor, and it is another thing to be a pastor with the responsibility and authority to make decisions affecting the congregants (decisions concerning the budget, contextualization of ministries, and more).

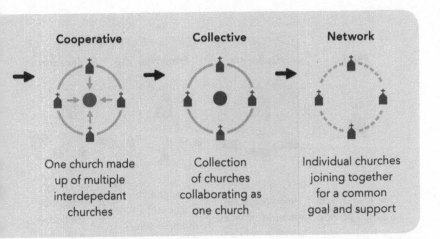

Cooperative	Collective	Network
One church made up of multiple interdepedant churches	Collection of churches collaborating as one church	Individual churches joining together for a common goal and support

Without such decision-making authority, a site should not be understood as a *church*—dependent, independent, or otherwise—but as a *campus*, despite the fact that it is in vogue for large franchise models to call their sites *churches*.

Why, then, do some models refer to their sites as churches? Often it's for practical, usually financial, purposes. It is more difficult to raise money for a campus than it is for a church. We saw this at Mars Hill in Seattle when they changed the nomenclature of their congregations from campuses to churches in 2011. The change did not reflect any revision in philosophy or practice within the church polity. Despite the change implying more autonomy, that was not the case. Arguably, at this time in the history of Mars Hill, it was the opposite. This change in nomenclature, regardless of motivation, appeared to be pragmatically driven. That is not always the case. Regardless of the motive behind the naming convention, we are advocating for nomenclature based on actual governance within the church.

By distinguishing between models based on the responsibility and authority to make decisions, we can consistently distinguish between the various models of multisite without trying to guess at the motivations or reasons for the various naming conventions. In addition, this way of organizing the models clarifies what we are proposing as a new classification: *multichurch*.

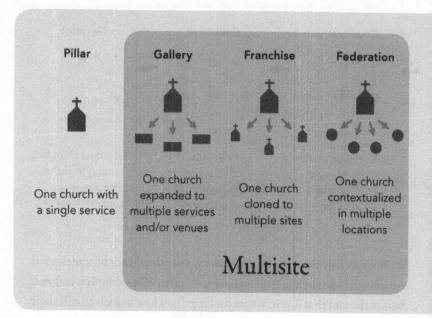

In the introduction we defined any church that that does not limit its gathering to one location and time as a multisite church. Therefore, the *multisite model* consists of one church that expresses itself in multiple *campuses* (multiple services, multiple venues, or multiple locations). We are proposing a further distinction from multisite, a natural evolution of the multisite model that differs from the earlier multisite models in where and how authority and governance are focused. We refer to these churches as multichurch. The *multichurch model* consists of one church that expresses itself in multiple *churches* that have a form of polity that provides the responsibility and authority to make decisions about budget, contextualization of ministries, and more.

If all of this feels a bit fuzzy and confusing right now, that's okay. In what follows we will explain these models in greater detail and illustrate the difference between multisite and multichurch on the spectrum of church models. Each model we discuss will be presented according to five aspects: description, examples, locus of power, strengths, and weaknesses.

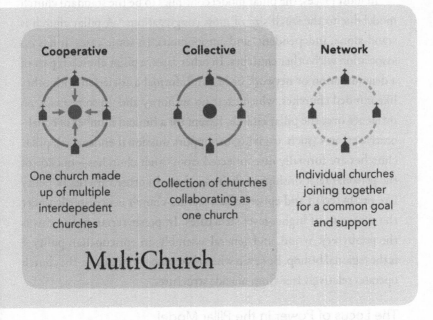

Cooperative

One church made up of multiple interdepedent churches

Collective

Collection of churches collaborating as one church

Network

Individual churches joining together for a common goal and support

MultiChurch

The Pillar Church Model

Before we begin looking at the various models of multisite and multi-church, we need to talk about a familiar model that is neither of those two: the pillar model. It is a stand-alone church with a single congregation meeting in a single service.

A pillar is a self-standing column, which is why we use the image to talk about one church with a single service. Until the explosion of megachurches with several services per Sunday, the pillar model was the most familiar. Studies demonstrate that just over half of US churches have one Sunday morning service.[2] Mark Dever's Capitol Hill Baptist Church in Washington, DC, is a good example. While this church does have connectivity through the Southern Baptist Convention and 9Marks,[3] it is driven by the single-gathering philosophy outlined in Dever's *Nine Marks of a Healthy Church*. Under this model, Capitol Hill has thrived, although its growth is limited—a limitation it enthusiastically embraces—by the size of the assembly space in which its members can gather.

In most places, the pillar model continues to be the standard church model due to the small size of most congregations.[4] A pillar church is stand-alone, independent, and autonomous. In some cases, it has no association with other churches. In other cases, a pillar church is part of a denomination or network or has an informal association with other like-minded churches, which exert no authority and, in some cases, no influence over the pillar church. Except for a limited number of collaborative efforts (such as giving to support missional endeavors), pillar churches are formally disconnected from other churches—outside of the personal relationships of their members. In other varieties of polity like presbyterian and episcopalian, a pillar church is necessarily under the authority of higher-level structures. In presbyterian polity this is the presbytery, synod, and general assembly; in episcopalian polity it is the regional bishop. But even when these associations exist, the church operates relatively free from outside structures.

The Locus of Power in the Pillar Model

In later models we will see that multisite and multichurch models feature a dynamic between central authority and local authority. The pillar model does not have the same tension. The locus of power resides in a pillar church's leadership—its solo pastor and board of deacons or its council (plurality) of elders, to give two examples. In a congregational polity, the membership also has a sphere of authority (approving/disapproving the budget and changing the statement of faith, for example). In the case of presbyterian or episcopalian polity, the presbytery or bishop enjoys a locus of power, but it is always seen as an external authority.

Strengths of the Pillar Model

One of the many strengths of the pillar model is the ability of the church to establish and control its own vision, worship, discipleship, mission, leadership, budget, and facilities. As we mentioned before, Capitol Hill Baptist under Mark Dever has been able to capitalize on these strengths to build a significant church in DC. A pillar church's ability to grow is a function of its ability and will to build larger facilities.

This control over its own direction serves it well. Even in presbyterian and episcopalian polities with their external authority structures, the local church authority is primary and functions similarly to pillar churches.

Additionally, a pillar church can contextualize itself for the neighborhood in which it is located. This allows such a church to tailor its aesthetic, music, components of service, and vision for community to reflect the cultural norms of its context. This is true of many historically black churches, such as Forest Baptist Church in Louisville, Kentucky. The structures a pillar church develops for its worship service, small groups, finances, and community outreach can be straightforward—nothing like the complexities inherent in the other models. It can have a unified, flexible, nimble, and focused church structure.

Moreover, when sufficiently small, a pillar model church fosters a strong, intimate fellowship. The ability to gather the entire congregation in one place at one time encourages a family gathering feel that can be lost in larger churches, especially when their members can no longer meet all together.

Weaknesses of the Pillar Model

The pillar model has been a mainstay of the church landscape for centuries, yet it is not without weaknesses. For the purposes of this discussion, we will limit our assessment of the weaknesses of the model as they relate to multisite. With this constraint in mind, we see the primary weakness of the pillar model is what it fails to provide as an autonomous church. The two most obvious limitations are isolation (which prevents deep collaboration) and the inherent restrictions on leadership development and growth.

The first limitation is isolation, or lack of collaboration. The Evangelical Baptist Church of Lugano in Switzerland was a pillar church. Filippo Zielke and I (Gregg) were copastors of this congregation of thirty-five people. We planned the worship services, took turns preaching, led Bible studies, and provided pastoral care. Everything was our responsibility. Structures were minimal, relationships within the church were close, and church life was . . . messy. As a church with a dozen nationalities represented, this was not a surprise. We were one church, with one location, with one service.

When our Swiss church tried to participate in a cooperative evangelistic outreach with other area churches, we lacked the vision and manpower to collaborate. Isolation also made it difficult to find the resources to help when we got in over our head. While our experience was exacerbated by the church's location in a predominantly secular culture, many churches choose the isolation inherent in the pillar model.

While independence has some advantages when it comes to efficiency, it can also be a very "lonely" model. Some pillar churches seek to overcome this weakness by joining efforts in their city or within a denomination, but collaboration and shared responsibility in leading are not inherent within the model. This can be especially critical in times of crisis.[5]

Crises can come in a myriad of ways, from getting overwhelmed by counseling cases to financial strain. One common example is a crisis related to the leadership of the church. We have seen several churches face challenges in dealing with charges against their pastor because of the pastor's isolation. The lack of support puts a heavy strain on the leadership and doesn't provide the safety or accountability possible with connectivity.

Overlake Christian Church in Seattle faced this challenge at the tail end of the 90s when charges were brought against its former lead pastor. As an independent church, it lacked the inherent safety of connectivity that would have provided a sounding board and wise counsel. Such support would have been invaluable during that time. While it has now reestablished itself as a healthy church, it took years to recover from what some would argue in hindsight were poor and avoidable decisions.

As for the second limitation, leadership development and growth are often casualties of the pillar model due to limited opportunities. Churches that don't provide opportunities for gifted leaders to develop in their congregations risk losing those leaders to other works or, worse, see their gifts atrophy from lack of use. While sending leaders to other works may be good for the kingdom, it is not a particularly successful strategy for the pillar church itself. Even pillar churches with a fairly healthy growth curve can saturate leadership needs fairly quickly because of the inherent limitation for multiple preachers and high-level leaders. In contrast, multisite churches grow at a rate five times faster than single service churches.[6] While growth is not the defining characteristic of health, it is an important factor to consider. Growth not only indicates the advancement of the gospel but also provides new opportunities for developing leaders.

Multisite

As defined earlier, a multisite model is one church that expresses itself in multiple *campuses*—multiple services (one version of the gallery model), multiple venues at the same location (a second version of the gallery model), and multiple locations where the one church is cloned (the franchise model). The following are expressions of the various multisite models.

The Gallery Church Model

The first variety of multisite is the gallery model. This model is one church in one location with multiple services and/or venues. Studies show that nearly half of all US churches have at least two Sunday morning worship services.[7] Many churches consider moving to this model for practical reasons. They have experienced growth and can no longer seat people in a single service, yet they aren't interested in building or buying a larger meeting space. Some churches also use this as an attractional strategy by offering different styles or expressions of worship and preaching in different services. These strategies are called "attractional" because they are intended to draw more people to the church and to Christ by meeting felt or perceived needs. Whether the gallery model is adopted as a temporary or a permanent solution, it is the most basic expression of multisite.

Why do we call it the gallery model? A gallery is a collection of shops under one roof. Accordingly, the gallery model consists of one church expanded to multiple services and/or venues. One variety is a *multiple services* church. As a pillar model church expands beyond its seating capacity for one service, it might add another service at a different time.

The two services are often (nearly) identical; only the meeting time is different. Alternatively, that church may seek to reach two different audiences. It expands from one to two services, and these two are quite different. For example, when Hinson Church moved from one service to two, the 9:00 a.m. classic service was primarily aimed at the church's senior population, and the 11:00 a.m. contemporary service targeted a younger crowd. As a two-service church continues to grow, it might add a third and a fourth service.

A second variety is a *multiple venues* church, or one church that expresses itself in multiple settings at the same location. While meeting at the same time at the same location, members may choose to attend a venue that features worship with jazz music, while others select a different venue that features country music for worship. In many cases, the church synchronizes and broadcasts the sermon via video at all the venues.

One example of a well-known gallery model with multiple venues is North Coast Church. Its Vista location in North San Diego County has ten different venues offering nineteen worship services on Saturdays and Sundays. As it explains, the Vista campus "features multiple simultaneous worship venues.... You can choose the style of worship that you like and still enjoy the same great teaching in every venue." These are

- *North Coast Live*, featuring a "full worship band and live teaching,"
- *The Edge Venue*, featuring "an edgier atmosphere for worship,"
- *Soul Gospel*, featuring "groove oriented, gospel centered music with a touch of soul,"
- *Sundays 4 Singles*, "a video venue sponsored by our singles ministry,"
- *The Message*, committed to "simply the message,"
- *Traditions*, featuring "a mix of classic hymns and old favorites,"
- *Last Call*, featuring an "extended, reflective worship time after the message,"
- *Encore*, which "features contemporary worship,"
- *Country Gospel*, featuring "gospel/bluegrass worship," and
- *Venue en Español*, featuring "live worship and teaching all in Spanish."[8]

A key characteristic of the gallery model is having one staff that leads multiple services. The emphasis of this model is on being one church while accommodating the needs (overcrowdedness) and wants (worship style) of different groups within the congregation.

The Locus of Power in the Gallery Model

Like the pillar model, and unlike the other models that follow, the gallery model has only one locus of power. Indeed, leadership for this model typically looks very similar to that of a pillar model church. The single, central leadership structure—whatever this may be (and it may vary significantly)—makes all the decisions, and the different worship services or the different worship venues express these centralized decisions.

Strengths of the Gallery Model

The gallery model is a creative solution to the problem of growth, and it is very useful as a strategy to engage diverse groups of people. It creatively replaces the costly solution of building a larger facility by using the same space for additional services. This is both efficient and wise stewardship. Sizing a building for one service often leads to a building design that is impractical for other uses during the week. This commits a significant amount of resources into a space used only fifty-two times a year. By offering different styles of worship in various venues at the same location, a church can more effectively attract a wide variety of people, thereby expanding the mission of the church. Additionally, for both multiple services and multiple venues, the simplicity of having one, unified staff is an important strength.

Weaknesses of the Gallery Model

Like the pillar model, the gallery model also has its weaknesses. By settling only in one location, the church limits its missional footprint within a city. What do we mean by a limited "missional footprint"? Simply that being in one geographic location has the potential to isolate the church as a destination that people travel to attend, rather than fostering an expression of the gospel throughout the city, contextualized to different neighborhoods.

Another weakness, as many gallery churches illustrate, is that multiple services and multiple venues cause division in the church: part of the membership attend the 9:00 a.m. service while others the 11:00 a.m. service, or part of them worship in the jazz venue while others in the country venue. In the latter case, when the division is defined by the members' experience, competition between the congregations at different services or venues can develop. This competition can be a distraction when it leads to arguments or disagreements over resources and staff.

In addition, there is always a danger that a consumeristic mentality may replace proper church unity, self-sacrifice, and service. By building services to accommodate personal preferences like a mall food court, we cannot avoid reinforcing consumerism. We cannot tell people that we can tailor church to meet their needs and then be disappointed when they demand their needs be met rather than seek out opportunities to serve.

Finally, as gallery model churches multiply services, the need for additional staff (each worship venue has its own pastor) and volunteers (each worship service needs children's ministry personnel) increases exponentially. Such expansion calls for careful budgeting so that staffing needs do not dominate to the detriment of ministry, mercy, and mission.

The Franchise Church Model

The second variety of multisite is the franchise model. This model focuses on cloning one church, and it is the model that most people think of when it comes to the multisite movement. A franchise is a business that is granted the responsibility and authority to market a company's goods or services. Suppose a company's product (such as computers) or service (such as care for the elderly) experiences some measure of success. The company distributes its brand—that product or service—through its licensed affiliates, or franchises. Working from this definition, the franchise model is one church cloned to multiple sites, each of which is granted the responsibility and authority to express the church's "brand," that is, its vision, worship, preaching, discipleship, care, and mission. Two distinguishing features of this model are the centralization of control and the management of the church's brand. In most cases, there is a third distinctive: the use of video or streaming to broadcast the sermons of the lead pastor.

Even though Mars Hill in Seattle closed its doors in 2015, it remains one of the most well-known examples of the franchise model. Willow Creek in Chicagoland is another well-recognized expression of this model. Others include Summit Church with J. D. Greer at the helm (Durham, North Carolina), Harvest Bible Chapel with James MacDonald as its leader (Chicagoland), Fellowship Church under Ed Young Jr. (Grapevine, Texas), Saddleback Church with Rick Warren (Lake Forest, California), Prestonwood Baptist Church under the leadership of Jack Graham (Plano, Texas), and Southeast Christian Church led by Dave Stone and Kyle Idleman (Louisville, Kentucky).

The Locus of Power in the Franchise Model

While both the pillar and gallery models have only one locus of power, the franchise model is the first model to distinguish between central and local authority. This split is always a source of tension in multisite and multichurch models. The central authority is typically a leadership team making and enforcing decisions to promote the brand (its vision, finances, staff, programs, etc.) for the cloned sites. The franchise model tends to be heavy on centralized leadership and brand management. This locus of power may reside in a lead pastor who is the founder and visionary of the church, or it can rest with an executive team. The use of video or streaming to broadcast the same sermon to all the sites centralizes the authority of the preaching of the Word of God. Decisions primarily come from the top down, flowing from the central authority that is responsible for the brand outward to the cloned sites. Still, some expressions of this model work hard to receive input from the leadership at the cloned sites.

With its emphasis on centralized leadership and brand management, the franchise model limits the decision-making ability of the local leadership. Managing the brand limits how far a local staff can diverge from the standard. In this, it restricts contextualization in favor of the brand. What authority is granted to local expressions typically resides in a local lead pastor or local elder team, which is given the responsibility to reproduce the brand at its site. Generally, neither the local pastor nor the local leadership team participates in the governance of the church through the central leadership team, yet some expressions of this model may incorporate the local leadership into their central leadership structure in creative ways.

Strengths of the Franchise Model

When a church is fruitful and growing, it is only natural for its leaders to want to replicate the conditions that produce that growth and effectiveness. This desire is often driven by a strong commitment to engage more and more people with the gospel and expand the church into new geographical areas. A strength of the franchise model is the addition of new worship services at sites that are not confined to one location unlike the gallery model. Furthermore, as a church replicates its brand, a proven reality is cloned at multiple sites. The rate of success is very high, the replication is easy, and the expansion is fast.

The model is also very attractive to the church membership because it provides a sense of unity through consistency. To draw an example from the business world, many people today like to be able to walk into the same coffee shop (Starbucks) or use the same service (Jiffy Lube) in different locations knowing exactly what they are going to get. Familiarity is calming and secure, and this model provides comfort and safety in a culture that is transient. Moreover, the limited need for local leadership allows a franchise model church to grow with less developed leaders. In this, it allows for leadership growth and development by providing opportunities for new and inexperienced leaders while not requiring them to have skills beyond their capacity. In particular, because of the centralized sermon by the lead pastor, the local pastors do not need to have well-developed preaching abilities.

Weaknesses of the Franchise Model

As we will discuss in more detail in chapter 4, the franchise model is susceptible to many of the common critiques of the multisite movement. One criticism is that the use of video preaching in multisite churches promotes idolatry. Digitizing one preaching pastor and beaming his sermon-bearing image into multiple sites fosters arrogance and pride. Add to this the highly publicized failures of several multisite pastors in recent years, and it does give credence to the idea that the franchise model is inherently susceptible to cultivating a cult of personality.

A second critique concerns the failure of the franchise model to effectively develop preachers and leaders. With centralized sermons and leadership, local pastors are not given sufficient opportunities to mature in their preaching and leading. Their role, while essential, is limited to shepherding and caring for their local members. This results in a continual exodus of younger leaders who look to other churches or organizations that give them opportunities to use their God-given gifts.

Another potential weakness of the franchise model relates to the idea of a brand that defines the identity of the church. There is always the danger that sticking to the brand takes priority over spreading the message of the gospel. When a franchise exports an entire brand, it sometimes does so in such a rigid manner that some sites are unable to embrace the brand because of cultural differences. In order for the vision, worship, preaching, discipleship, care, and mission to be tailored to multiple sites, many of the elements of the brand must become fairly generic, lacking a contextualized approach. This "generic" approach emphasizes the lowest common denominator for unity and can result in less impact for Christ as the church detaches from the culture where the site or campus is situated. One of the key criticisms of the franchise model is that it is more deeply rooted in secular notions of branding than in the Scriptures.

The Federation Church Model

The federation model focuses on being one church that is contextualized in multiple locations. A federation is an organization made up of smaller or localized organizations. A key difference between the federation and the franchise models is that federation models employ *live preaching* at every (or almost every) location, and the different locations have local elders and staff. This enhances the church's ability to contextualize the gospel and provide more effective leadership at the local level.

A federation model church has both shared (centralized) staff *and* local staff for each location. The centralized staff provides support for campuses in ways that maximize efficiency and reduce administrative burden. Federation churches are often led by executive teams that establish vision and provide day-to-day management of the church. In these models, many management decisions, including staffing and budget, are still determined centrally and presented to campus pastors. However, there is distinctly more freedom to contextualize at the local level—in everything from the sermon preached on Sunday to how the ministry allocates spending.

A federation model church may develop out the franchise model in an effort to address some of the weaknesses of the franchise model. This can happen as the managers at the cloned sites mature into strong leaders and seek greater flexibility and freedom to deviate from the brand of the franchise. If the central leadership of a franchise model church is willing to empower campus pastors, it can make the transition to the federation model. Each campus pastor must own the overall vision of the church while capably adapting it to their particular context. This model is dependent on church leaders understanding the importance of contextualization and possessing the skills to adapt the gospel and its expression in different places. The central leadership team urges, supports, and celebrates this contextualization, while the leaders at the multiple locations carefully contextualize the one church according to, and for the sake of, their different demographics.

Though it is beyond our purpose to address contextualization in depth, it can be helpful to clarify what we mean by this term. Pastor Tim Keller of Redeemer Church in New York City says that contextualization "is giving people *the Bible's answers*, which they may not at all want to hear, *to questions about life* that people in their particular time and place are asking, *in language and forms* they can comprehend, and *through appeals and arguments* with force they can feel, even if they reject them."[9] According to Keller, contextualization requires a number of skills, including the ability to exegete the Scriptures, study and understand the culture in which the church exists, and creatively and winsomely communicate the message of Scripture and the gospel in ways that people in that culture can understand. It is a missionary task and one that is biblically warranted, even demanded.

As I (Gregg) have said elsewhere, "Contextualization is seen in Peter's Old Testament-rich proclamation to his Jewish audience on Pentecost (Acts 2:14–41), Paul's simple words to the peasants of Lystra (14:8–18), and his address to the philosophically sophisticated Athenians (17:16–34)."[10] Flowing from the contextualized gospel is the adaptation of the church in different cultures in terms of its worship, discipleship, mercy, care, and mission.

The founding documents of The Gospel Coalition, a network founded by Keller and his friend Don Carson, further explain the need to contextualize the gospel for fruitful ministry: "The gospel itself holds the key to appropriate contextualization. If we over-contextualize, it suggests that we want too much the approval of the receiving culture. This betrays a lack of confidence in the gospel. If we undercontextualize, it suggests that we want the trappings of our own sub-culture too much. This betrays a lack of gospel humility and a lack of love for our neighbor."[11] While contextualization is certainly wrought with difficulties, neglecting contextualization is simply not an option for churches that take the Great Commission seriously. This is one reason why the emphasis on contextualization in the federation model—as well as in the cooperative and collective models—is necessary and proper.

Several churches around the country employ the federation model, including Veritas Community Church (Columbus, Ohio), Apostles Church (New York City), and Brentwood Baptist (Brentwood, Tennessee). Each of these churches is a multisite church that features live preaching at their various sites.

The Locus of Power in the Federation Model

Some of the locus of power in the federation model resides in an executive team that is responsible for the governance and management of the church as a whole. This team is responsible for establishing vision, developing the budget, and managing the staff. This usually includes determining staffing and budgets for local campuses as well. In many federation churches, this central team provides vision and oversight for essential ministries that are expected to be available to each campus. This team is often made up of staff from local campuses with the local bodies and the central authority sharing the staff's time.

Despite significant central control, federation model churches share some responsibility and decision making with the leaders at the multiple locations—certainly more than a franchise model church. These local leaders exercise their authority in conjunction with the executive team, which encourages and commends contextualization at those locations. This authority for contextualization is exercised through the pulpit, through the various ministries of the church, and through some budgetary autonomy.

Strengths of the Federation Model

The federation model shares many of the strengths of the franchise model—as one church expanding its mission by cloning itself at multiple sites—while also encouraging greater contextualization at those locations. Whereas the franchise model tends to emphasize the promotion of the church's brand (and this point does not discount the centrality of the gospel to this brand), the federation model highlights the expansion of the gospel and its expression—the church—contextualized for different people in multiple locations.

The federation model also has some very practical benefits in developing leaders. Campus pastors have more opportunities to exercise their gifts as leaders by expressing their ownership of the church's vision, adapting the church in their multiple locations, and developing their preaching gifts and other leadership skills.

Weaknesses of the Federation Model

When the federation model's balance of power is tipped toward its centralized leadership, it suffers from many of the same weaknesses as the franchise model. A strong centralized leadership that fails to empower local leadership can discourage new leaders, and like the franchise model, there can be a tendency to promote the brand over and against contextualization.

Because the federation model lies between the franchise model and the two multichurch models, it exists in a "no-man's-land," where campus pastors taste some freedom but are frequently frustrated with feeling micromanaged. This particular weakness makes the federation model difficult to sustain for long periods of time, especially when local sites develop strong and capable leaders. As we will discuss further in chapter 8, the financial cost of the central control tends to increase some of the frustration that campus pastors feel in this model.

Finally, as we saw with the franchise model, the federation model finds it very difficult to maintain balance in the locus of power. As a practical matter, many churches that give more freedom to local sites end up having to standardize the vision, worship, preaching, discipleship, care, and mission to maintain unity, effectively impeding the church's impact across different demographics.

Multichurch

As indicated by our focus on the locus of power in the church, there are many strengths and weaknesses to the various multisite models. Tensions develop as churches seek to balance centralized authority and governance with the desire to contextualize the gospel to local congregations and give greater freedom to local leadership. This tension leads us to the next generation in the evolution of the multisite movement: the multichurch model. As noted earlier, the *multichurch model* features one church that expresses itself in multiple *churches* that have a form of polity that provides the responsibility and authority to made decisions about budget, contextualization of ministries, and more. The first variety of this model brings together multiple interdependent churches as one church (the cooperative model). The second is a collection of independent churches collaborating as one church (the collective model). We will take a look at each of these in turn.

The Cooperative Church Model

The first multichurch model on the spectrum is the cooperative model. A cooperative model is multichurch because it is one church composed of multiple interdependent churches. Moreover, the level of interdependence between the churches is fairly substantial. It is the degree of interdependence among the churches that distinguishes it from the collective model, in which largely independent churches collaborate.

The cooperative model of multichurch is similar to the business model that goes by the same name. A cooperative (or co-op) is a business or organization made up of people that voluntarily cooperate for their mutual social, economic, and cultural benefit. These members, marked by interdependence, act in concert toward a unified goal. When applied to the structure of the church and our discussion of the multisite spectrum, the cooperative multichurch model features one church made up of multiple interdependent churches.

This model strikes a balance of control between the centralized and local leaders by having a leadership council composed of pastors representing their respective churches as well as some shared staff. The local leadership teams of these churches are composed of pastors and staff, and these teams develop and execute their respective contextualized visions, always in conjunction with a shared vision that is determined collectively through the central leadership council. Their interdependence as one church is expressed in a variety of ways, including a shared theology, vision, and philosophy of ministry. Some cooperative multichurches have a common liturgy for their worship services and a common approach to discipleship, while others have joint mission and mercy ministries or other centralized services. This is a brief summary of the model, but we will discuss this model in greater detail in section 2.

The Locus of Power in the Cooperative Model

In the cooperative model the central leadership focuses on the broad, long-term vision and the management of central functions. The governance of the church as a whole is shared between local and central leaders who form a board or leadership council. The members of the board may include some with special roles as executive elders, whose primary concerns are the overall vision and core values of the church. The board also includes the pastors of the various local churches, whose concerns are the contextualized expressions of that vision and the core values for their respective demographics. There may be other leaders included as well, such as nonstaff elders, whose concern is to mediate between the executive elders and the pastors of the churches when either the centralized leadership or the local leadership threatens to dominate the church.

At the local level, authority resides with the local pastors, staff, and their respective elder teams. Consciously working in conjunction with the leadership council, this team contextualizes the overall vision, worship, mission, discipleship, mercy, care and more for the particular demographics of their location. Unlike the federation model, this team has budgetary authority for spending and staffing along with the freedom to contextualize the vision locally.

The church that we, as authors, belong to is an example of this model of multichurch. For many years, Sojourn Community Church operated within the federation model and has recently evolved into the cooperative model. As a federation model church, Sojourn was deeply centralized in terms of its preaching (though not broadcasting sermons, the four speakers for Sundays preached the same text and worked with a fairly standardized outline), liturgy, community groups, discipleship, children's ministry, pastoral care, missions, mercy, and women's ministry. Staffing was centralized so that these ministries were led by central staff pastors or directors. Finances were also centralized. All the money given to Sojourn's four campuses was pooled together, then distributed back to the churches for staffing and ministry needs. Financial decisions, including the budget allocations to the four campuses, were largely made by the executive leaders with limited input from the four campus pastors.

As the four campus pastors developed strong gifts of preaching and leadership, became proficient at contextualization in their respective locations, and struggled with the heavy-handed centralized locus of power, Sojourn found itself in a position to transition into a cooperative model of church. This began with the creation of a leadership council that addressed both centralized and localized concerns through representation at those levels. Sojourn established a structure that strives to achieve a balance between control and ownership, elements traditionally in tension with each other.

Strengths of the Cooperative Model

If there is one word that sums up the strength of this model, it's *balance*. More than the other models, the cooperative model seeks to achieve a balance between control and ownership. To accomplish this balance, there are several systems in place to avoid, on the one hand, a blatant abuse of power and, on the other hand, a stifling of initiatives through micromanagement. The same is true regarding the balance between the one church's vision and core values and the contextualization in and through the multiple churches. The model seeks sufficient ownership of the common mission to ensure a significant degree of similarity between the various churches, matched by sufficient freedom given and creativity encouraged to ensure a proper contextualization. In section 2, we will take a more exhaustive look at the advantages of this model; therefore, we keep our comments here brief.

Weaknesses of the Cooperative Model

Of course, the bane of theoretical balance is that the balance is never fully achieved in practice. As in any cooperative model, balance shifts back and forth as the various checks and balances operate over time. This is true of any governmental system, of course. Consider the American system of federalism that seeks to balance the interests of the states with a central federal authority. The divisions of power and authority into three branches and the checks and balances designed into the structure help to preserve balance over time, but at any given time the balance is shifted in one direction or another. You never achieve that perfect balance. Likewise, the cooperative model suffers from the normal and constant tension between central and local authority and between the overall vision and its actual contextualized expressions.

Other weaknesses include the complexity of the cooperative model, the increased time commitment that interdependence demands, and the higher risk for leadership conflict between the central structure and the local churches.

The Collective Church Model

Continuing to the right end of the spectrum is the collective model. A collective model church is a multichurch because it is a collection of individual churches. Though these churches are largely independent, they collaborate as one church. It is this unifying factor that distinguishes the collective model from the network model on the far right of the spectrum.

A collective is a group of individuals working together on a common project without relying on internal structures. Members of a collective, marked by a limited similarity, compose the one group with a unified commitment to sharing power and authority. A collective multichurch is a collection of largely independent churches—equal partners—collaborating together as one church. Located to the right of the cooperative multichurch, the collective model possesses the least amount of centralized leadership and grants the most autonomy to the local churches. Despite this high level of independence at the local level, these churches cooperate in a limited number of ministries and share a limited number of resources. In some cases, these churches are former sites of a multisite church or are church plants from the original congregation.

Redemption Church—"one church in ten local congregations across the state of Arizona"—is an example of the collective multichurch model. It has a very limited central governing structure, as they explain on their website:

Central Operations are structured to support and empower local congregations in the freedom that has been given to them. This is done by efficiently meeting common needs with centralized leadership, freeing congregations of the burden to dedicate energy, resources, and/or staff to meet those needs locally. Central Operations are intentionally minimal to reduce the financial burden place on the local congregations, who contribute a percentage of their budget to fund it. Currently in Redemption Church, facility maintenance, media and communications, legal and finance, and Outward Focus Ministries (missions) are part of Central Operations. Central Operations provides a tremendous support structure for the birthing of new Redemption congregation.[12]

Clearly, Redemption Church's balance of power is strongly tipped toward the leadership teams of the ten congregations, each of which has freedom to contextualize its efforts. These are independent churches collaborating together.

The question of how these congregations are unified is answered by their commitment to four categories of boundaries, which help to

define the space in which local congregations have freedom to contextualize their ministry. These boundaries are meant to empower leaders with clarity, direction, and resources rather than limit them with constraints. They are in place to help the multiplication of healthy disciples and leaders who do the work of ministry in their local church.[13]

These four main categories of boundaries are as follows:

1. Covenant: We are bound together as one legal entity with shared resources.
2. Beliefs and practices: We operate from the same foundation in the gospel.
3. Culture: We have shared values and expectations.
4. Communication: We speak the same language and present a consistent message.[14]

Thus, the unity and collaboration are centered on relationships, resources, theology, values, vision, and speech, with an outward focus on the multiplication of new Redemption Church congregations.

The Locus of Power in the Collective Model

Because the collective model emphasizes local independent churches in cooperation with each other, central control and authority are intentionally kept to a minimum. Centralized leadership that includes significant representation from the collaborating churches fosters relationships between those churches, provides resources for them (such as finances, communications, legal services, and human resources), imparts common vision and shared values, and encourages multiplication. A minimum percentage of the collaborating churches' budgets is contributed to support the work of the central leadership team.

Freed of the burden to take care of the many administrative tasks that are part and parcel of the responsibilities of pillar model churches, collective model churches dedicate their staff, resources, time, and effort to worship, discipleship, pastoral care, mercy, and mission. These churches, led by their respective leadership teams of pastors and staff, possess the requisite authority to engage in these ministries in a contextually sensitive manner. They delegate the responsibility for finances, communications, and other administrative structures to the central leadership team and have representatives from their local church on that team.

Strengths of the Collective Model

For many pastors, what makes this model attractive is the delegation of many of the normal church administrative tasks to a central operations team. This frees up the pastoral leadership to focus on preaching, discipleship, and having gospel conversations with members of their local congregations without the added pressure of taking care of hiring and training staff, keeping up facilities, seeking legal counsel, and the like. Two other strengths are that a limited percentage of the local churches' budget is contributed to central operations, and the intentional cooperation among those churches is limited to multiply like-minded churches. Again, we will delve into the strengths of the collective model as well as the cooperative model in section 2.

Weaknesses of the Collective Model

A weakness of this model is that its success is largely dependent on avoiding conflict between the local church leaders. The minimal level of expected collaboration and contribution to the collective (as contrasted with the cooperative or other multisite models) is such that each church could easily spin off from the collective as an independent church. While this could be considered a strength, it can also require additional time and energy to maintain healthy relationships among the leaders. This is similar to some of the weakness of the cooperative model, but the greater independence of the local churches in the collective model can also mean less accountability. Conflict resulting in high turnover could be substantially disruptive to the mission of the church.

Additionally, the low cost for churches to participate in the collective model necessarily limits the resources and services that the central collective can provide. This leads to role duplication in each local church, more than might be necessary, and it can lead to inequality among churches in the collective. In this model there can be significant disparity between staff compensation, ministry funds, and facilities depending on the demographics of the local congregation.

We found this to be the case for Redemption Church, as compensation and ministry budgets vary significantly between collective churches as a function of location and demographics. For them it is part of their story, but it can be frustrating for staff, requiring more effort to maintain unity. This also means that members' experience will be vastly different based on which church they attend. For example, within a collective church it is common to find a well-funded children's ministry in a church situated in an affluent suburb and a spartan version of the same ministry at a more economically challenged location. Members may not understand the disparity and may find it difficult to move between churches as they transfer homes or jobs.

Network Churches

To the far right of our spectrum is the network model. Because the partnership aspect of this model is quite limited—with a single concentration on church planting—it is neither multisite nor multichurch. Still, the network model is included on the spectrum because it shows a further step between a central authority and local congregations.

A network implies the concerted participation of individual churches that band together for a limited purpose. Pillar model churches may partner with other churches as part of a network; thus, it is possible to bend our spectrum into a circle. That being said, the pillar model is driven primarily by the desire for autonomy while a network is built for connectedness, though intentionally limited. The contrast between these models places them on opposite ends of the spectrum in regard to authority. On the left, there is the complete control of the pillar church because there is only one organization, the church itself. On the right, the control of the network exerts little authority over individual member churches.

In this way, the network model is slightly different from the other self-contained models already presented. It is included here because as you move across the spectrum toward less centralized authority, you eventually cross the line toward independent churches. A network represents the transition from one church to several independent churches that still maintain connectivity.

A network is a system of people or organizations interconnected for a purpose. When the independent churches are functioning well, a network accomplishes more than the sum of the parts—in this case, independent churches. Here we have individual churches joining together for a common goal and for mutual support for greater fruitfulness in mission and ministry.

Dave Harvey, speaking with regard to church planting, explains that "a network is churches partnering for mission by or through message, men, model, and money."[15] The apostle Paul emphasizes this type of partnership when he thanks the church in Philippi for their "partnership in the gospel" (Phil. 1:5). This was a church that participated with Paul in his imprisonment and in defense and confirmation of the gospel (Phil. 1:7). This type of collaboration was *external* to the church through an association with Paul and consequently, through Paul, with other churches that supported his missionary efforts to launch new churches.

Network churches give a percentage of their budget to support common church-planting initiatives. They pool other resources as well, such as prayer, training, and expertise in areas like pastoral care and sermon preparation. In the past two decades, the growth of networks, especially for church planting, has been startling. Networks include Acts 29, Redeemer City to City, Sojourn Network, Summit Network, Pillar Network, and Church Multiplication Network, to name a few.

The Locus of Power in the Network Model

In keeping with the reduction in the central locus of power of the previous multichurch models, the network model has the least amount of centralized authority. A network is often led by a board of directors made up of leaders from the network churches. This centralized board has authority to execute a very limited range of activities. For example, it may collect the individual churches' network giving, distribute it to support church planters and their ministries, accept new churches into the network, and assess potential church planters. When an individual church is not carrying out its commitments to the network, the board has the authority to remove it from the network. The sole authority of the network's centralized leadership is to promote the common cause. Typically, they do not get involved in the internal decisions of individual churches unless the churches seek advice as they would from a friend.

This means that everything else pertaining to the individual churches is under the leadership of the local locus of power. Local churches have their own vision, part of which includes network initiatives. They make their own decisions about worship, discipleship, care, and mission priorities, some of which may extend to efforts beyond those of the network.

Strengths of the Network Model

Networks have significant strengths. They attract like-minded leaders who band together in a brotherhood that energizes the common cause. Most networks are highly relational and missional in focus. Many younger leaders, frustrated by the bureaucracy and stagnation of denominations, are joining these more informal networks. Additionally, because networks are focused on a limited number of initiatives, their leadership structures and administrative costs are minimal. Low administrative costs enable them to devote a high percentage of their budget to a specific purpose—church planting, for example. This is one reason why the network model has grown and has proven to be effective in recent years.

Weaknesses of the Network Model

That said, the model also has its weaknesses. If we consider some of the recently initiated networks, their staying power is a big concern. How will they weather the storms caused by failed church plants, disagreements among members, church transitions, or other challenges that accompany organizations with diverse leaders? Will they still be around in another twenty years? Some traditional denominations are critical of networks because they now do some of the things the denominations used to do so well. When churches opt out of denominations and join a network or when denominational churches dually align with a network, financial support for the denomination may suffer.

Conclusion

The spectrum of churches encompasses a wide range of models, from the nonmultisite pillar model to the beyond-multichurch network model. In between, as the locus of power shifts from centralized authority toward local authority, we move from multisite (the gallery, franchise, and federation models) to multichurch (the cooperative and collective models). For each model, we have presented its description, examples, locus of power, strengths, and weaknesses.

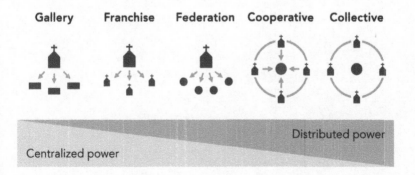

Now it's your turn! As you consider each of the models, where does your church fit? Consider the strengths and weaknesses. Where do you see the locus of power in your own church? Is that a strength or a weakness?

In addition we encourage you to consider if your current model is still a good model for what your church wants to be and do. Is there a better model to which your church should transition? Before we dig deeper into the different models on the second half of the spectrum (the multichurch models that represent the next generation of the multisite movement), we will first take some time to address some of the additional concerns with the multisite church movement. In the next chapter we will interact with the most common critiques and evaluate each of the models we have discussed in relationship to these criticisms.

4

Landmines

Now that we have some clarity about the various models of multisite and multichurch, we want to dig more deeply into the concerns with the movement and the various models. The multisite movement is still relatively new, and the success of this rapidly developing phenomenon has attracted supporters and critics. The tenor of the critiques range from friendly engagement to aggressive opposition. We will treat them with appreciation, as iron sharpening iron, to the degree that these criticisms are aimed constructively at challenging multisite churches to think critically and biblically about their structure.[1] Rather than dismiss the criticisms of multisite models, our desire is to thoughtfully consider the challenges and determine if we can improve the existing multisite models for the greater health of the church.

As we evaluate the types of critiques made over the past two decades, one issue seems to dominate the discussion: the question of video and, specifically, to what extent it is acceptable to use video in the multisite model. Because this issue attracts the greatest amount of criticism, we have organized the objections into two main categories: objections targeted at franchise models relying on video, and a collection of more general concerns regarding the various multisite models.

The Biggest Objection to Multisite:
Video Franchises

We address the challenges to the "video venue" model in their own section because an unusually large number of the critiques of the multisite model are directed at this particular expression of multisite. The four specific criticisms can be summarized in this way:

1. Video venues foster a cult of personality.
2. Video venues devalue the pulpit and preaching of the Word.
3. Video venues neglect the care of the congregation.
4. Video venues isolate the preacher from the congregation.

We will consider each of these objections in turn.

Cult of Personality

Those who are critical of video multisite churches often argue that the use of video promotes idolatry. Digitizing one preaching pastor and beaming his sermon-bearing image into multiple locations—throughout the city, the extended metropolitan area, the country, or even the entire world—fosters a cult of personality. Some critics go as far as to argue that using video leads to the stimulation of pride, arrogance, and self-promotion, thus contradicting the biblical values of humility and self-deprecation. They believe any pastor and/or church that cultivates such attitudes is necessarily ungodly. Often, this criticism is accompanied by the recognition that small single site churches can also foster a cult of personality. A rural church of thirty-five members can certainly make the error of elevating its pastor and feeding his pride in an idolatrous way.[2] Still, critics make a distinction here by claiming that the degree of accountability for the pastor is greater in the small church than it is in a large multisite church. Thus, it is less likely for idolatry to take root in a single site church than a multisite church. This leads such critics to the conclusion that multisite is both wrong and dangerous because it promotes idolatry and pride.

We understand why some make this criticism of multisite churches, and we won't deny that examples of such idolatry are available to illustrate the problem. But we want to underscore something that can be easily overlooked. Idolatry, pride, arrogance, and self-promotion are first and foremost a matter of the heart and not a function of a church model.

These dangers are certainly not confined to the multisite church models. Church history is replete with examples of single service churches falling prey to the cult of personality. This danger has plagued the church since its inception, as the early church also showed a tendency to rally around its favorite preachers: Paul, Apollos, Peter, and Christ (1 Cor. 1:12). This underscores the point that the danger of a church falling into a personality cult resides in the followers' propensity to elevate a leader as much as it resides in the leader's desire to be elevated.

Does this mean that we should uncritically adopt video and the use of video venues? The use of video certainly presents some unique challenges. It cannot be denied that projecting a pastor's face on a ten-foot-wide screen in four locations can feed his ego and tempt him to believe that he is in some way uniquely the source of his church's success—despite the clear word of Jesus on that matter (Matt. 16:18). When we couple this with the efficiency of multisite models in promoting growth, we have a strong basis for critique. While pride and success are variables that must be addressed in every church regardless of how many services they provide and how many people they reach, we do agree that video venues must be approached with additional care.

Therefore, because idolatry and pride are sins that infect Christians generally and pastors in particular, this charge against multisite calls for action. We encourage those who are considering the use of video to evaluate two areas before adopting this model. First, all churches should follow Paul's presentation of the qualifications for pastors in 1 Timothy 3:1–7 and Titus 1:5–9.[3] Elders should meet and continue to grow in the qualifications established for the pastoral office. Preachers and leaders should be called by the Holy Spirit and should be men of character, competent in teaching, leadership, prayer, shepherding, hospitality, correcting, and discipleship.

One of Paul's directives to pastors demands particular attention in this situation: "He must not be a recent convert, or he may become puffed up with conceit and fall into the condemnation of the devil" (1 Tim. 3:6). When a new (or immature) Christian becomes a church planter or the pastor of an already existing church, it can be an invitation to trouble. The task of preaching, providing pastoral care, leading, and the other ministries of being a pastor can encourage the sinful attitudes of idolatry, pride, arrogance, and self-promotion. These can find a greenhouse for cultivation in any successful ministry. Even the apostle Paul had a thorn in the flesh to help him to remember his dependence on Jesus and his own weakness apart from Christ (2 Cor. 12:7). The end of this trajectory, if left unchecked, is tragic. "Puffed up with conceit," the young church planter or immature pastor falls into condemnation, repeating the pattern of the fall of Satan who, when inflamed with pride, was expelled from the presence of God in heaven (1 Tim. 3:6; Jude 6). For this reason, when looking for leadership in planting and pastoring, churches should seek spiritually mature leaders who have demonstrated humility and ask for accountability from others

Still, this doesn't mean that churches should prohibit young or relatively new believers from moving into pastoral positions or engaging in church planting. What should be done in these cases? And, of course, even spiritually mature church planters and leaders may be lured into idolatry by their successes. What should be done to avoid such temptations?

This is where the second area is needed: a call for accountability. Churches need to develop structures that regularly evaluate a planter or pastor, properly reward fruitfulness and faithfulness in life and ministry, honestly underscore weaknesses and failures, and offer correction with oversight in those areas. This is not unique to any of the models. Such accountability in either a pillar or multisite model may formally entail the elders or a team of both pastors and lay members doing an annual evaluation of the lead pastor. Informally, a lead pastor's openness to critique and rebuke can be fostered through deep friendships with other elders. In recent years, many lead pastors (whether multisite or pillar model) have begun to eschew such accountability as outdated or unnecessary. To the degree leaders avoid accountability within their own church, people should avoid following their leadership. A pastor's vulnerability with the church's members and his refusal to be placed on a pedestal can go a long way in staving off pride and selfish ambition.[4]

Ultimately, we agree with the concern that using video sermons increases the chances of developing a cult of personality, even if it is not always the result of this particular model. Still, concerns about idolatry and pride, when approached biblically and holistically, should be salient warnings for video multisite churches. When considering a multisite model, churches should recognize the inherent temptation in this model to elevate leaders, and should appropriately design structures to mitigate against this tendency.

Devaluing the Pulpit

A second concern about the use of video in the multisite model centers on preaching. There are two aspects to this objection. First, because the preaching pastor's sermons are digitized and broadcast to the various campuses, video multisite churches are "nonincarnational." In other words, the preaching is done by a disembodied man on a screen, which some critics consider an illegitimate means of preaching.

Support for this stance is rooted in a broader biblical theology recognizing that God did not just send words to save the world; he sent his Son as God incarnate—God in the flesh—to rescue us. Additionally, there is a strong link between Jesus's preaching and his healing ministry. Jesus both announced the good news of the kingdom and demonstrated its arrival through exorcisms, healings, resurrections, and more. Moreover, Scripture insists that good works accompany sound doctrine. For example, after urging Titus to "teach what accords with sound doctrine," Paul further encourages him to "show yourself in all respects to be a model of good works, and in your teaching show integrity, dignity" (Titus 2:1, 7 ESV). These and other biblical passages are taken to signify that sermons are to be delivered by pastors who are *present physically* as they preach. The idea of the regular, weekly projection of God's Word via a virtual pastor to a congregation seems inconsistent with this incarnational emphasis.

In response, those who advocate for video multisite churches may question the legitimacy of the conclusions regarding preaching from these biblical passages. Some have responded by arguing that God has frequently used culturally relevant means to address his people. For example, the Mosaic covenant was structured according to treaties in existence at that time (using an existing secular medium), and Paul wrote letters like

Romans and Colossians to announce the gospel to people he had never personally met.[5] Furthermore, we need to recognize that technology is constantly changing and improving to the point where "advancements in technology make it such that the telepresence of the preaching pastor is so vivid that he can actually engage with the audience, and they with him."[6]

Still, video multisite churches should give attention to this concern and acknowledge that virtual preaching is *not* the same as preaching in person. This raises the question of whether the sermon is somehow changed, or even distorted, by being broadcast. With any technology, we need to think carefully about how the medium we use in communicating affects the way that message is received. Our experience shows that there are legitimate concerns with broadcast video preaching, most notably, that the pastor forgoes the particularity of address and application in order to appeal to a larger, less particular audience. In the franchise model, because the pastor is speaking to congregations spanning various contexts and cultures, he must generalize the message in order to broaden its appeal. What, then, is the impact—short-term and long-term—on a congregation receiving such generalized messages? What is the effect of having a disembodied pastor preach digitized sermons?

There is a second aspect of this critique that we need to consider. Video multisite churches tend to suppress the development of other preachers by focusing on one or two charismatic communicators. If the one pastor whose sermons are broadcast to multiple sites preaches on the vast majority of Sundays, little room is left for other pastors to preach and thus advance in their communication abilities. As one critic summarizes, "For every additional [video] multi-site campus out there, there's one less preaching pastor being raised up for the next generation."[7] Jamus Edwards's research demonstrates that over half of the campus pastors in multisite churches desire one day to serve as a senior pastor with preaching responsibilities.[8] To answer this critique, video multisite churches might respond by saying that those they attract to be their campus pastors are gifted in areas other than preaching. They use their gifts of teaching, shepherding, exhorting, mercy, and so forth by leading ministries at their specific campus. For example, they might lead the pastoral care, community groups, or mercy ministries at their campus. Though they are able to preach and teach (1 Tim. 3:2), they lead in other ways, while the one preaching pastor for all the campuses does the bulk of the preaching.

Our own experience reinforces this concern and supports the critique that video venue models reduce the opportunity and motivation to develop preachers. The reliance on video is often done as a nod to the skill and charisma of the broadcast preacher, but such attitudes—even when they are well-intentioned and done to reach more people with the message—end up locating the power of the gospel in the communicator rather than in the gospel itself. We do not deny the effect of a strong communicator, nor are we advocating that churches should open their pulpit to anyone who desires to preach. However, to avoid the concerns of cult of personality, we encourage the development of multisite pastors who preach to their particular congregations.

It should be noted that the concern about devaluing the pulpit can also be directed at a solo pastor in a pillar model church. The thinking is that each church should have one pastor and that pastor should be the (main) preacher. If that is the case, how does a solo pastor promote the development of other preachers? Doesn't a solo pastorate suffer from the same weakness as the video multisite church, if not more so? Moreover, in many churches where there is a plurality of elders, not all the elders are regularly preaching. A few will typically do most of the preaching, as warranted by Paul's instructions about double honor (reputation and remuneration) for those elders who frequently preach, a subset of the church's full council of elders (1 Tim. 5:17). Accordingly, this criticism is not unique to video multisite churches. In many other types of churches, the preaching skills of anyone other than the solo pastor or a few elders are not developing.

Still, we believe the criticism has some merit. In response, we urge video venue churches to address some of these challenges by giving campus pastors the responsibility to preach occasionally. Although the campus pastors will not preach as often as the lead pastor, whose sermons are transmitted to all the campuses, they will preach occasionally, thereby developing their communication ability. Alternatively, video venue churches can develop a teaching team so that various pastors preach the sermons broadcast across the campuses. Additionally, campus pastors who sense the call to devote themselves to preaching should be encouraged to plant churches or to become the lead pastor responsible for preaching at another church. If a multisite church has been blessed by a campus pastor's ministry of counseling, mercy, community, and the like, releasing that campus pastor to take on preaching duties elsewhere might reciprocate the blessing.

In sum, we find the concerns regarding the preaching of the word through video venues to be valid. Disembodied messages and inattention to developing preachers are legitimate failings of the video model. In these ways the video model devalues the pulpit by diluting the message and limiting the messengers. We strongly encourage video multisite churches to evaluate their ability to communicate the gospel in an embodied form and to consider how to prepare the next generation to proclaim the gospel.

Neglect of Pastoral Care

The responsibilities of the campus pastor expose the weakness of a third critique commonly made of video multisite churches: they suffer from an inability to provide pastoral care, prayer, loving community, and discipline. In our study of multisite churches, virtually all of them address this concern and are committed to providing the full range of pastoral oversight and church ministry at all their campuses. The fact that the campus pastors do not preach regularly on Sundays does not mean they are inactive or unable to provide pastoral care and support in other ways. On the contrary, the campus pastors of whom we are aware frequently work with a team of staff and volunteers to exercise leadership in counseling, community group development, children's ministries, youth ministries, outreach, prayer, mercy ministries, church discipline, and other ministries of the church. In addition, the resources available at each campus are potentially available for other campuses to use if needed. This sharing of resources reflects the strong collaboration desired and envisioned by multisite churches.

We agree that the preaching pastor whose sermons are broadcast to all campuses *does not* also provide pastoral care to every member of the church. This is true not only in multisite churches that use video sermons but also in churches that do not. Additionally, churches with a solo pastor who does everything can expect pastoral burnout, poorly functioning ministries for which the pastor is not gifted, and a spectator mentality among its members. This is not a healthy church. Where there is a plurality of elders who lead and minister, some elders will dedicate themselves to preaching, some to providing pastoral care, some to extending concrete help through mercy ministries, some to community discipleship, and the like. We find this approach to be very similar to a multisite structure, and in later chapters we will argue that the multichurch model actually fosters leadership development through the expansion of ministry into multiple congregations.

While there are likely some multisite churches that use video and neglect the pastoral care of their members, we could not find any concrete examples of it and have to conclude that we do not see this critique as having merit. Often this concern is leveled at multisite models based on the assumption that leaders of large video venues do not care about their people, but in practice we have found that this is rarely the case. Even in examples of unhealthy churches where lead pastors fail or are removed from their position, the churches are usually filled with pastors who love their sheep and strive to care for them. Contrary to this concern, we have found good evidence that video multisite churches can provide adequate pastoral care to their various locations.

This was certainly the case at Mars Hill. Although it was a large video venue franchise church, I (Brad) never doubted the love my fellow pastors and staff had for the members of the congregation, and I never doubted their commitment to provide care. Opinions will vary as to the effectiveness of such care, but great effort was taken to build care structures and programs such as community groups, counseling, and redemption groups.[9] Regardless of the method used for sermon delivery, pastoral care was a priority for Mars Hill.

The Isolation of the Preacher from the Congregation

Finally, the fourth critique of the use of video preaching in a multisite church is really a conglomeration of issues that we have grouped together, all relating to issues of intimacy and accountability. The first criticism is that the use of video preaching makes it difficult, if not impossible, for the preaching pastor to know all the members of his congregation. In addition, video multisite seems to prohibit the effective exercise of church discipline because a member who has been excommunicated at one location can simply go to a different campus and hide anonymously. Related to this second point is the broader concern that the multisite model makes it easier for members to be anonymous. Many of the critics of multisite acknowledge that these and similar criticisms can also be leveled against large churches that are not multisite. Therefore, the concerns are really broader concerns about how to effectively care for and discipline members in large churches.

Those who advocate multisite respond to these criticisms in several ways. First, they point out that the assumption behind the critique seems to be that the ideal is a solo pastor model in which one pastor knows each and every member of his congregation. While this is certainly a wonderful thing, it only works in a fairly small church. More to the point, however, is that this idea—that the ideal church is a single pastor who knows all the members—seems to inhibit the development of leadership structures needed for a healthy church. In the Old Testament Moses is actually rebuked for trying to pastor every member of his congregation. Indeed, he is challenged to establish "capable men" to lead what are essentially multiple congregations among the people of Israel (Ex. 18:21). In the early church the apostles did the same thing, choosing additional men to spread the responsibility of leadership so they can better focus on "prayer and the ministry of the word" (Acts 6:1–7). These examples are reflected in the plurality of elders model that many churches adopt. In this structure, a church can grow very large while maintaining intimacy and accountability, if the number of pastors grows in a corresponding way. The health of the body is not dependent on having a single lead pastor who knows each and every member of his church. Rather, the full council of elders together bears this responsibility.

Similarly, in a video-based multisite church, the health of the body is not dependent on a single pastor whose sermons are broadcast to the various locations. He does not need to know all the members at every location. Rather, the elders at the different sites bear this responsibility together. The same is true of multisite churches that do not use video but have one (or more) pastor who dedicates himself to the regular preaching of the Word. The principle is the same in each context. It is not the local lead pastor's responsibility alone to know the people in his congregation. Rather, the congregational elders together bear this responsibility.

But can church discipline be done effectively in a multisite structure? Consider the situation of a member who, after being excommunicated from one location, attends another location without being recognized and reprimanded. Has this happened? Yes, we know of cases where this has happened. However, we think the solution is rather straightforward: the leaders at one location inform the leaders at the other location(s), alerting them to be on the lookout for excommunicated members. While this can be neglected, this responsibility is borne by all churches, whether they are linked as a multisite church or not. It is common to hear of a member who has been disciplined at one pillar church simply crossing the street to become involved in another church without the leaders at either church being aware of the situation. If anything, the multisite model increases the chances that the needed communication will take place between leaders. The effectiveness of proper church discipline depends more on the diligence of church leadership than on the model itself. It is important for multisite churches to develop these communication channels, but this is not a unique issue for the model, so it should not deter one from adopting the model.

The third objection picks up a general point from the last objection: multisite makes it easier for members to be anonymous. This critique assumes that multisite churches take a lackadaisical attitude toward membership, permit their members to be disengaged, and have no structures in place to ensure active participation by members. Do some multisite churches treat membership in this cavalier manner? Certainly, it is possible. Most of the multisite churches that we have worked with, however, are not ambivalent about member care. Indeed, with those we have worked with and studied, the membership requirements are quite rigorous, with elders and/or deacons interviewing prospective members to assess their level of commitment to the church covenant. Membership is often dependent on a certain level of involvement, like participating in a community group in addition to attending the weekly service. In most cases, attendees are regularly challenged through sermons and personal conversations to participate in these smaller community groups in which there is a high level of accountability. Many churches have a process for following up with members who appear to disengage or have fallen through the cracks.

That being said, it is always possible for people to stay anonymous if they do not want to be known. This challenge is definitely greater for larger churches where it is easier to hide. But again, this is not unique to the multisite model. A single service church of eight hundred people has a much greater opportunity for anonymity than an eight-hundred-member multisite church meeting in four locations with equal attendance at each site. It's much harder to avoid community in a church of two hundred than in a church of eight hundred.

While many of the critiques in this section are leveled at multisite in general, they are often directed at a caricature of video venue multisite churches. This is not surprising considering the attention these models have attracted in recent years. It is common to hear the criticisms that these models foster a cult of personality, devalue the pulpit, neglect pastoral care of members, and lead to isolation of members from leaders and from one another. We find some merit regarding the first two critiques, and there are lessons to learn in the latter two. To the extent that these critiques are on target, multisite churches should consider the recommended changes and take steps to rectify the problem(s). Yet we do not see them as sufficient reasons to reject the model entirely.

Other Concerns

While the loudest criticism tends to focus on the use of video in preaching, not all multisite churches use video. In this section, we turn to additional concerns that apply to multisite models in general. These concerns are about the use of branding, how to transition leaders, the governance of the church, a philosophy of pragmatism, and how the church meets or gathers together.

Branding

A common critique of multisite models is their excessive focus on branding and franchising the church.[10] This criticism says that the expansion of one church into multiple locations is another example of the church following the world in utilizing unbiblical models and methods. In this case, the church is mirroring the franchise business model of McDonald's or Starbucks, with each venue focused on reproducing the brand. At the heart of franchising is a push for numbers, size, influence, competition, and fame. Critics argue that a "merchandising and market monopoly spirit" drives multisite expansion.[11] Moreover, this approach fosters a consumerist mentality among church members, encouraging them to "shop around" to find the franchise offering them the best programs to meet their needs.[12] Churches promoting such values contradict Scripture and do not honor God.

This criticism is rather sharp and situationally appropriate. What we mean is that multisite churches motivated by a "merchandising and market monopoly spirit" should be avoided. To the extent a church locates its faith for growth in its franchising and when the brand is emphasized more than the gospel, we should be concerned. In some cases, pastors engage in platform building because they have come to believe *they* are the brand. As pastors we are shepherds, stewards, disciplers, and ambassadors, but we are not the brand responsible for selling God's church to the world.

At the same time, this criticism can be overstated. We have met with the leaders of many multisite churches whose emphasis on branding is not a means to sell the church. Instead, it is an evangelistic tool used to establish a unified identity. While it is fair to disagree with seeker sensitive strategies, we should be honest in acknowledging that the motivation is not always nefarious or self-seeking. Developing a particular corporate identity as a church body is unavoidable whether the branding is intentional or it is just allowed to happen without design. Branding in itself is not sinful, and in our experience, the motivation to franchise the church for personal gain is rare. Such criticisms often neglect to take the time to understand the church's actual motivation. Again, we have found that many multisite churches are spurred on by a holy passion to multiply gospel-centered congregations in order to reach their city for Jesus Christ. Rather than calling upon people to travel twenty minutes to one centralized location, they launch and develop new congregations throughout their city, fostering missional engagement where members live and bringing the church into the neighborhoods of nonbelievers.

Are we are concerned about the recent emphasis on branding? Yes. Within our church spectrum, branding tends to be more pronounced at multisite churches that adopt a franchise model, which emphasizes greater central control and authority. We should not utilize branding uncritically, and we encourage all forms of multisite and multichurch to evaluate their branding strategy and the motivation behind it.

Transition of the Preaching Pastor

Another concern relates to the question of leadership transitions. What happens to a multisite church when its founder exits, whether from retirement, death, moral failure, doctrinal error, or moving to another church? This problem is not unique to multisite churches; it is a concern for all churches. Whatever steps are commonly taken to ensure a smooth transition in churches in general may also be adapted for multisite churches. We believe that every church should have a succession or "backup" plan in case of the unexpected loss of the lead pastor.

The concern is amplified when a multisite model is dominated by one key leader in whose hands most, if not all, authority resides. In such cases, when that leader implodes, the problem of transition is one problem among many, and it is usually preceded by an unbiblical governance and authority structure that demonstrates a lack of pastoral accountability. One recent example is Mars Hill Seattle, which dissolved from one church with numerous campuses when its leader resigned amid controversy. Certainly, the transition from this one centralized church to nearly a dozen fledgling autonomous churches was rough, but a host of factors contributed to this difficulty. While there are many lessons to be learned from this example, the key point we want to emphasize is the need for a well-considered transition plan.[13]

Governance of a Multisite Church

Not all of those reading this book are under the conviction that a church should be congregationally led, but for some readers this will be an important issue. Some opponents of the model have argued that the multisite structure effectively prevents the church from being congregational. They claim that the multisite model does not allow for ultimate authority to reside in the congregation's members, the defining element of congregationalism. Members do not vet and approve elders. They do not vote on the budget and the sale and purchase of buildings. They are not responsible for receiving and, in the case of church discipline, excommunicating members. The elders make all the decisions—those just listed and all other decisions. When applied to multisite churches, the term *congregational* is a misnomer.

This objection is directed at certain congregational models of multisite, namely, those that are *elder-ruled*. In such models, we would agree that the congregation has no direct authority. Elder-ruled multisite churches should stop describing their governance structure as congregational. It is not. However, the elder-ruled system of governance is not the only model of government employed by multisite and multichurch models.

In *elder-led congregational* multisite models,[14] elders are responsible for and exercise their God-given authority over elder-level ministries. These responsibilities include leading the whole church, teaching and preaching, praying (especially for the sick), and shepherding the members.[15] Deacons are responsible for and exercise their God-given authority over deacon-level ministries, such as community groups, men's and women's ministries, mercy, and children's ministries.[16] Members are responsible for and exercise their God-given authority over congregation-level matters, among which might be approving leaders, voting on the budget, confirming the buying and purchasing of buildings, affirming changes to the constitution and bylaws, and receiving and excommunicating members. Some of these decisions—such as the vetting and approval of deacons—might be the responsibility of only one congregation. Other decisions—such as the affirmation of the annual budget—might be the responsibility of all the members in the various congregations. In this model of multisite, using the term *congregational* to describe its governance is legitimate and accurate. This line of thinking equally applies to the charge that multisite churches are inherently episcopalian[17] or presbyterian in polity.[18]

In light of this criticism, multisite congregational churches that are elder-led should carefully enumerate the responsibilities of their elders, deacons, and members. The congregation should exercise its authority in the designated areas, and the elders should not infringe on those congregational responsibilities—and vice versa. Ultimately, elder-led, deacon-served, congregation-affirming multisite churches are properly congregational.

An Unhealthy Focus on Pragmatism

Another common criticism of multisite is its focus on pragmatism or the justification that "it just works." When a multisite church has a captivating vision and quality leaders engaged in ministry, and it multiplies numerically and expands geographically to new locations, it is seen as highly successful. This success encourages the leadership to applaud itself and serves as a defense from detractors. "If you don't like what we do, just look at the numbers, the budget, and our multiple locations! It just works."

Pragmatism is not a stable foundation for any church, much less a multisite church. The church is the people of God; therefore, it is not our place to decide why it exists, what it does, and how it is organized. God's revelation in Scripture must dictate what the church is and does. Since the church is the body of Christ, he must command what the church is and does. The church is the temple of the Holy Spirit, so his guidance must direct what the church is and does. Scripture discloses that the church is a people, a body, and a temple. The Word of God has much to say about the essence of the church. Because we live in a highly pragmatic American society, multisite churches need to guard against defending their mission, vision, and structure with pragmatism.

One reason why pragmatism is dangerous is because culture changes, and what is currently "working" successfully in multisite churches may change as our culture changes, rendering the models ineffective and unsuccessful.[19] One way that multisite churches can guard against this ever-shifting pragmatism is by gauging their "success" according to the biblical metrics of faithfulness, fruitfulness, unity, purity, missions, and doxology. Honest self-assessment or, even better, evaluation from an external source such as a multisite church in the same denomination or network, can be helpful.

A church that is growing and successful because it employs a multisite strategy is not *necessarily* motivated by pragmatism. It is actually good stewardship to employ strategies that work and have been submitted to Scripture, the Spirit of God, and the lordship of Christ. Many multisite churches that we surveyed are faithfully engaging their members in God-honoring worship, leading them in discipleship, equipping and sending them on mission, serving their communities with mercy, and exercising discipline when needed. Proponents of multisite claim, and statistics confirm, that most churches that adopt a multisite structure do so for biblical and missional reasons: "The primary motive behind the multisite approach is to obey the church's God-given directives. The Great Commandment (Matt. 22:37–39) is to love God and one another, the Great Commission (Matt. 28:18–20) is to make disciples of all nations, and the Great Charge (1 Peter 5:1–4) reminds us to involve all believers in ministry."[20] That this biblical faithfulness leads to missional fruitfulness is a cause for rejoicing—not criticizing.[21]

The Church Cannot Assemble Together

A final objection is that multisite churches, while indeed following one part of the biblical pattern of being distributed into various locations, break the biblical pattern of the whole church gathering together. That is, multisite churches exemplify the gatherings of the church of Jerusalem in the disciples' homes, but fail to reflect the assembly of that church in the temple, with all its members meeting together in that one location.

Framing the objection in this way helps to avoid the hypercriticism that "a multi-site church formally removes the concept of 'assembly' from the definition of 'church' since it's a church that never actually assembles."[22] In truth, a multisite church does assemble in each of the locations in which its members gather together to worship, hear and respond to the Word read and preached, pray, give, confess sin and acknowledge divine forgiveness, baptize, celebrate the Lord's Supper, and more. Multisite churches do indeed assemble.

To temper this criticism, many multisite churches choose to occasionally gather together as a whole assembly in one location. These regular meetings may be, for example, quarterly congregational/business meetings, or specific worship gatherings on Christmas Eve, Good Friday, Ash Wednesday, and/or other liturgically significant days. But how many of these gatherings are enough to satisfy the need to assemble? In addition, many other multisite churches never gather together, for a variety of reasons. Some see no need to come together, or they are too big to gather in one location because it is cost prohibitive and logistically difficult to rent a facility (e.g., a sports stadium or a convention center) in which the whole church can meet. For others, even when all the members gather together, multiple services are needed to contain them all in any meaningful way.

At the very least, this criticism is a helpful challenge to multisite churches that, when they are physically able, they should attempt to meet together as the whole church. As Brian Frye urges, "Multi-site churches should attempt to gather the entire church body periodically as the context allows."[23] Such an application reflects the biblical pattern of the early church both gathering together and meeting in the disciples' homes. To paraphrase Frye, if the dynamic of small churches alongside a larger church fostered strong spiritual growth of believers and exponential expansion of converts in the early church, then a similar pattern should be endorsed for multisite churches.[24] Even though we believe that the weekly gathering of local congregations in multisite models meets the biblical admonition to assemble, we still encourage these churches to assemble as a whole church when able.

Conclusion

In this chapter we have listened to critics and placed the multisite movement under the microscope, submitting it to common objections and critiques. Our desire in doing this is to explore the appropriate challenges these criticisms raise. In many cases the concerns are born out of a love for God's church and a passion for faithfully advancing his mission throughout the world. Engaging with these concerns rather than dismissing them outright challenges us to thoughtfully and carefully lead our churches. Our conclusion is that some multisite models do raise significant concerns, yet the multisite movement in general looks good under the microscope. Church leaders should always be willing to learn from criticism, and a fair analysis of the criticism shows that solutions are possible within multisite and multichurch models.

The lessons we have learned provide a valuable service to the multisite movement, and the creative impulse that has driven the movement has also been hard at work refining structures and models to better address these concerns. In fact, many of these refinements have led to the birth of new models, including the multichurch expression we highlight. This new model of multisite is an answer to many of the challenges and criticisms that have called for a more biblical and effective model. In other words, multichurch is the evolution of multisite. In the next chapter, we will explain why we believe it is the future.

The Future

As we look back on our journey into this new frontier of ecclesiology called the multisite movement, we have presented a spectrum of seven models of church and weighed numerous concerns about multisite. In this chapter we turn to a discussion of *why* we believe multichurch is the future of multisite. To be clear, this is not to say that current multisite expressions will not endure or that they are all inherently flawed. However, we do expect to see more and more churches adjusting to the challenges multisite models create. In many cases as multisite leaders continue to refine their churches in accordance with biblical convictions instead of pragmatism, we believe they will transition their churches to the new multichurch model.

Biblical and Theological Convictions

Before we begin to evaluate the benefits of multichurch, we first need to explain our motivation. We are focused on and driven by three biblical and theological convictions. First, we believe that the church is an organism rather than an organization. Second, we see the church as an image-bearer. And third, we know the church is the body of Christ. Let's look at each of these in more detail.

The Church as an Organism

In a book about models and systems, it would be easy to conclude that all this discussion is about the best organizational structure. But that would place the emphasis on pragmatic concerns by asking "What's most effective?" Instead, while the church does have many characteristics of an organization, we believe that Scripture presents the church of Jesus Christ as an *organism* rather than an *organization*, as something alive and organic rather than a program or structure.

Indeed, the church is imaged as a *people* (1 Peter 2:10), a *family* (Eph. 2:19; 1 Tim. 5:1–2), a *body* (1 Cor. 12:12; Eph. 4:15–16), a *flock* (John 10:16; 1 Peter 5:1–3), and a *bride* (Rev. 19:7; 21:2). What these metaphors have in common is that they are living things. Even when inanimate objects are used to refer to the church, they are pointedly modified. When Paul presents the church as a temple, he emphasizes that it is the temple of the *living* God (2 Cor. 6:16). Peter expands this vision to include church members as *living stones* being built into a spiritual house (1 Peter 2:5).

The church of Jesus Christ is an *organism* composed of living beings who belong to the living God. Thus, to reduce the church to a mere *organization* consisting only of systems, structures, and policies is an affront to the biblical presentation of the church. Understanding the living nature of church keeps us dependent on the Spirit of God as we lead the church and build structures.

This should not be understood to suggest that structure is irrelevant, however. It is not a question of choosing one or the other; it is a matter of prioritization in defining the essence of the church. Structure is still necessary for the health of living things, and the church has many organizational components. In *The Trellis and the Vine*, Colin Marshall and Tony Payne underscore that while the vine (i.e., the church ministries of evangelism and discipleship) is paramount, the trellis (i.e., the administrative work) is needed to support the vine.[1] Articles of incorporation, constitutions, bylaws, policies, structures, programs, staff hiring and evaluations, finances and budgets, planning, and meetings galore are significant and necessary. These elements provide support for the living nature of the church.

The Church as Image-Bearer

When we think of the church as a collection of living people, it also helps us to see it through the eyes of God. He views the church as a living organism made up of his redeemed image-bearers, and the purpose of image-bearers is to reflect and represent as much truth about their subject within the limitations of the medium. In our case, the medium God has provided is our creatureliness. As image-bearers, our purpose is to mirror and magnify the truth of God as much as we can within our limitations as created beings. So we live, we enact, and we speak this truth. Breathing, creating, laughing, weeping, encouraging, resting, preaching, teaching, working, loving, and everything else we do has the ability to reflect and represent the one, true, living God.

What is true of us individually is also true of us collectively. After deliberating about the creation of man in his image (Gen. 1:26), God actualized his plan: "So God created *man* in his own image, in the image of God he created *him*; male and female he created *them*" (Gen. 1:27 ESV).[2] *Man* (grammatically singular), or the whole of the human race (conceptually plural), was created in the divine image. Then, "male and female he created *them*" (grammatically plural), referring to the individual male human being (conceptually singular) and the individual female human being (conceptually singular). Individuals reflect and represent God as his image-bearers, and humanity as a collection of people reflects and represents God as his image-bearer.

What is true of people in general is particularly true of people who have been rescued from sin through Jesus Christ. Referring to the church, Paul affirms, "For we are God's handiwork, created in Christ Jesus to do good works, which God prepared in advance for us to do" (Eph. 2:10). The idea of "handiwork" is that of "the skillful work of a craftsman" or, according to the New Living Translation, a "masterpiece."[3] As the handiwork of God created to do good works, the church is to reflect and represent the truth of who God is and what he has done. Just like individual image-bearers, the church taken altogether is a collection of redeemed people and is also God's image-bearer. As "chosen people, a royal priesthood, a holy nation, God's special possession," the church exists to "declare the praises of him who called you out of darkness into his wonderful light" (1 Peter 2:9). Beyond proclamation of the truth of God, the church is also the personification of the true God, so that when unbelievers "accuse you of doing wrong, they may see your good deeds and glorify God on the day he visits us" (1 Peter 2:12). The church is the redeemed image-bearer of God.

The Church as the Body of Christ

Scripture uses another powerful metaphor for this collection of redeemed people: a body, specifically, the body of Jesus Christ. As Paul explains, "Just as a body, though one, has many parts, but all its many parts form one body, so it is with Christ. For we were all baptized by one Spirit so as to form one body—whether Jews or Gentiles, slave or free—and we were all given the one Spirit to drink. Even so the body is not made up of one part but of many" (1 Cor. 12:12–14). As he baptizes new Christians with the Holy Spirit, Christ incorporates them into his body. Accordingly, Christians are members of one body. As Paul continues to explain , the parts of the body are dependent on one another for their collective health and for the ability to accomplish the good works designed by God (1 Cor. 12:15–27). They are many parts, all of which are important and each with its particular role to play. One part cannot opt out of the body; that would render the body incomplete. Some of the parts cannot reject or despise the other parts; such a lack of equal concern for other parts would lead to division of the body.

This body metaphor, with its emphasis on the unity and collective activity of all body parts, underscores the reality of the church as fundamentally relational in nature. By divine design, the parts are interdependent and thus act together in concert. Only in this way can the body—the church of Jesus Christ—grow and flourish as a living entity.

As we consider the benefits of a multichurch model, we are driven by these three biblical and theological convictions: the church is an organism rather than an organization, the church is image-bearer, and the church is the body of Christ. We understand the church to be an organism that was created by God to be his image-bearer and that is being built as the body of Jesus Christ to reflect and represent the truth of who God is and what he has done. This truth should be sung and prayed through the church's worship, proclaimed in its pulpit, displayed by its discipleship, expanded through its mission, and—most importantly—reflected in its very essence. The church's organization (its systems, structures, policies, and methodologies) must serve the church as organism, image-bearer, and body.

The Assessment of Multichurch

These biblical and theological convictions should lead us to favor models of the church that not only allow for but also explicitly promote the church's ability to flourish as an organism, reflect clearly the image of God, and operate as a healthy body. We believe biblical and theological conviction, rather than pragmatism, should drive our thinking about, and embrace of, these models. While this point may seem obvious (after all, it is the church we're discussing), experience has shown that it is very easy for the church to settle for pragmatic solutions when making decisions about leadership and structure. The expanding diet of leadership and business books being devoured by church leaders has only exacerbated the problem. Again, our point is not that lessons learned from the business world should be avoided or that we keep doing ineffective things because we are convinced they are the only biblical way to do them. The insights we learn from the business world, sports, history, and other fields can be helpful and have their place when appropriate. Our point is that the church is the creation of God, and therefore, God's Word should receive priority in the building of church structures and governance. Lessons from these fields of study are useful when we consider organizational matters, but the organization must serve the organism. The institution must aid the image. The business must promote the body.

Why are we spending so much time on this issue? Because we have spent countless hours rehearsing this matter with churches that have stumbled into multisite models, not because of biblical or theological convictions, but because they were in search of answers to pragmatic problems. In many cases the church's leadership team chose a multisite model to solve short-term problems, but they failed to consider the trajectory on which their decision had launched the church. We have spoken with many churches of different structures and theological convictions about their elder teams, membership, financial models, training classes, and so on—all of which were tied in knots because the churches had not fully considered their multisite model and methodology. Avoiding these problems begins by leading from our convictions. We should be driven by conviction about what God says rather than pragmatism, and we should lead with the confidence that we can develop a model that enables the church to reflect and represent the truth about God and his ways both internally (its nature and values) and externally (its structures and policies).

As we have said several times, we think that multichurch is the future of multisite. We believe this to be the trajectory because the multichurch model and methodology leads to a church structure that best expresses and accomplishes the vision of a conviction-driven organization. So how and why do multichurch models accomplish this? We turn to Scripture for the answer to that question. In Ephesians 4:1–16 and its presentation of God's goal for the church, we find seven implications for the church's structures and methodologies. In the structure and governance of the church, we want to foster unity in the body of Christ, differentiate between unity and uniformity, advocate presence over proximity, cultivate collaboration, promote diversity and thriving, overcome ecclesiological reductionism, and encourage multiplication.

Here is the text of Ephesians 4:1–16 that forms the basis for these implications:

> As a prisoner for the Lord, then, I urge you to live a life worthy of the calling you have received. Be completely humble and gentle; be patient, bearing with one another in love. Make every effort to keep the unity of the Spirit through the bond of peace. There is one body and one Spirit, just as you were called to one hope when you were called; one Lord, one faith, one baptism; one God and Father of all, who is over all and through all and in all.
>
> But to each one of us grace has been given as Christ apportioned it. This is why it says:

"When he ascended on high,
he took many captives
and gave gifts to his people."

(What does "he ascended" mean except that he also descended to the lower, earthly regions? He who descended is the very one who ascended higher than all the heavens, in order to fill the whole universe.) So Christ himself gave the apostles, the prophets, the evangelists, the pastors and teachers, to equip his people for works of service, so that the body of Christ may be built up until we all reach unity in the faith and in the knowledge of the Son of God and become mature, attaining to the whole measure of the fullness of Christ.

Then we will no longer be infants, tossed back and forth by the waves, and blown here and there by every wind of teaching and by the cunning and craftiness of people in their deceitful scheming. Instead, speaking the truth in love, we will grow to become in every respect the mature body of him who is the head, that is, Christ. From him the whole body, joined and held together by every supporting ligament, grows and builds itself up in love, as each part does its work.

Unity in the Body of Christ

The first and preeminent concern of this passage is church unity.[4] The church is summoned not to create but to *maintain* its unity, which is itself a gift from the Holy Spirit through the bond of peace. The church should enjoy being united, yet because of its members' sins of pride, divisions, and selfishness, the gift of unity is disturbed and can even be destroyed at times. The church must exert a concerted effort to reject factions and cultivate the unity God has granted it.

In this task, it is aided by seven commonalities:

1. The church is one body, which is the people purchased by Jesus Christ.
2. The church is the temple of God's one Spirit.

3. The church has one hope, which is the eternal life to which it is called.
4. The church has one Lord, Jesus Christ, who is the only mediator between God and man (1 Tim. 2:5).
5. The church has one faith, which is the sound doctrine that the church confesses.
6. The church has one baptism, which indicates repentance from sin and faith in Christ as the proper response to the gospel.
7. The church confesses one God and Father of all, who is the Creator and Sustainer of his image-bearers.

Furthermore, right attitudes and actions on the part of its members serve the maintenance of the church's unity. Humility is having the proper assessment of oneself and considering others to be more important than oneself. Gentleness is strength in meekness refusing to use power for personal gain. Patience is persistence through trials and testing that threaten to destroy unity. And bearing with one another in love is enduring the shortcomings and idiosyncrasies of the other members of the church and then giving oneself to them. Inasmuch as the church is characterized by these commonalities and expresses these attitudes and actions, it maintains its Spirit-given unity.

Counterfeit Unity

It is very important to understand this call to unity rightly. The church is not urged to achieve *uniformity*, but to maintain *unity*. These are two different callings. *Uniformity* is about being identical, having a sameness that defines and characterizes you and others. This sameness can be mandated through the use of power, control, and standardization. For example, if uniformity is a multisite church's emphasis, then each service or site (as with the gallery model), or each location (as with the franchise model), should be nearly the same. Uniformity is also evident in one sermon being preached at multiple services or being broadcast at multiple locations. Other aspects of uniformity may include standardized children's and youth programs, community group structures, and the manner in which pastoral care is done.

Unity is not the same as uniformity. *Unity* is about being made one as various parts are combined or ordered to promote a common identity. Using the body metaphor, the church is a unity as Jesus Christ redeems people and incorporates them into his body, and the Holy Spirit joins together these diverse parts through the bond of peace into one whole. Unity cannot be coerced or programmed. Rather, it requires the Spirit's work to link together the parts, the church's work to fight against divisions and eagerly maintain unity, and the members' work to be humble, gentle, patient, and forbearing in love.

While unity can be maintained in any church model, we appreciate how the multichurch models intentionally presses churches toward an eagerness to maintain unity. The multichurch configuration itself requires maturation in the leadership as well as the structures of the organization. While some may contend this is risky, we would argue it is more dangerous to live under a false sense of unity within the church. This is highlighted in Ephesians 4 when we are told it is through unity that churches become mature. The pursuit of uniformity is frequently carried out through power, control, and standardization, resulting in sameness; the pursuit of unity is done through a Spirit-conferred peace, a Spirit-given eagerness, and a Spirit-empowered life, resulting in very diverse parts being combined to form one body. As a result, the maturity this body attains is far greater than the maturity the individual parts could attain alone. When this is applied to multichurch models, it teaches that the maturity that can be attained by one church that unites multiple interdependent churches (the cooperative model) or multiple cooperating independent churches (the collective model) is greater than the maturity that one church on its own can attain. Likewise, the level of maturity attainable by multichurch models is greater than the maturity attainable by multisite models, which emphasize uniformity over unity.

Artificial Presence

As we noted in chapter 4, one of the principal objections to multisite churches is their failure to assemble, either regularly or at all. To put it positively, we agree that churches should be places where members are physically present with one another. Although we disagree with the primary criticism of multisite, namely, that the entire church must gather at the same time, we do not deny the importance of presence. While we do not believe that the use of video (or other technologies, like telepresence) for broadcasting sermons can be categorically prohibited, we do not see it as an ideal or preferred method.

Our reason for this concerns the difference between *proximity* and *presence*. *Proximity* is the state of being near. A message that is broadcast or a hologram that is projected approximates proximity. When it is done well, it can give the appearance that the person speaking on the screen is near. Although we are thankful for the technology that allows us to video chat with our kids when we are away, it is clearly not the same as being present with them.

On the other hand, *presence* requires embodiment and relationship. We are embodied, relational beings created in the image of a relational God. As such, we naturally desire to connect, not just observe. As Bonhoeffer says,

> The believer feels no shame . . . when he yearns for the physical presence of other Christians. Man was created a body, the Son of God appeared on earth in the body, he was raised in the body . . . and the resurrection of the dead will bring about the perfected fellowship of God's spiritual-physical creatures. The believer therefore lauds the Creator, the Redeemer, God, Father, Son, and Holy Spirit, for the bodily presence of a brother. The prisoner, the sick person, the Christian in exile sees in the companionship of a fellow Christian a physical sign of the gracious presence of the triune God.[5]

To the people of his church, God gives pastors and teachers to shepherd, care for, and lead them to deeper relationship with Jesus. In our culture, we have turned this idea on its head, building churches as if God gives people to the pastor to increase his clicks, likes, and platform. Congregations need pastors, with all their strengths and weaknesses, to be present with them. They need to connect with the human reality of their leaders: "This is what it is to be a leader: to bear the risks that only you can see, while continuing to exercise authority that everyone can see. . . . Only those who have opened themselves to meaningful risk are likely to be entrusted with the authority that we all were made for and seek."[6] While many maintain they can be satisfied with the rehearsed, edited projection of an ideal pastor, the church will not be better for it.

We have great respect for technological advances in the realm of transmission, videoconferencing, mobile collaboration, and telepresence, and we have been the beneficiaries of these remarkable developments. Still, the end they aim to achieve is always a virtual presence. That qualifier "virtual" underscores the key difference between the technologies of proximity and the actuality of presence. Ephesians 4 reminds us that we should value presence over proximity. Why? Because this passage underscores the presence of Christ in relationship to the Father and the Spirit (from whom he descended and to whom he ascended) and Christ's presence in relationship to his image-bearers (for whom he descended and from whom he ascended). We were not given a virtual savior or something approximating a real human being when God became incarnate. We were given a real person who had a real presence in this world. The Son was both incarnate (embodied) and lived in a specific location (emplaced). Following his ascension, Christ's presence fills "the whole universe" (Eph. 4:10). To the church Christ gave more than gifts. He gave gifted people—apostles, prophets, evangelists, and pastors and teachers—to equip its members for ministry, and this giftedness requires presence.

Again, while we do not categorically reject broadcasting sermons and employing telepresence, we believe that multisite churches that use these means are irregular, though not heretical or sinful in this practice. These means achieve a proximity between the message and members, but fall short of the presence of a flesh-and-blood messenger bearing the message to the church. We do not deny that these means exert influence and effect transformation as they achieve proximity, but we believe that the church's need for presence cannot be replaced by solutions that offer mere proximity. It is most fitting that the church's gifted people be a presence, and as they are present to the church, they exert influence and effect transformation relationally. Rather than trying to figure out how to *seem* present by using technology that helps the church to grow and mature, we seek to build the church by presence: people who are present and who relationally press the church toward multiplication and maturity.

Cultivating Collaboration in a Multichurch

The preeminent benefit of the multichurch model is the collaboration it forges between churches. This may surprise some who are tempted to see the greatest advantage in the efficiency of sharing costs and reducing staff. Unfortunately, we have found this "advantage" to be a myth, and we will talk more about it in a later chapter. In reality, collaboration—not efficiency—is the primary benefit of the multichurch model.

Leaders who have planted churches on their own, even if attached to a network or a denomination, need little convincing of the importance of collaboration. Even most pastors of existing churches experience tremendous isolation and long for a collaborative ministry to remove the loneliness. In *Life Together*, Dietrich Bonhoeffer discusses the importance we have for one another in the Christian life:

> But God has put this Word into the mouth of men in order that it may be communicated to other men. When one person is struck by the Word, he speaks it to others. God has willed that we should seek and find His living Word in the witness of a brother, in the mouth of a man. Therefore, the Christian needs another Christian who speaks God's Word to him. He needs him again and again when he becomes uncertain and discouraged, for by himself he cannot help himself without belying the truth. He needs his brother man as a bearer and proclaimer of the divine word of salvation. He needs his brother solely because of Jesus Christ. The Christ in his own heart is weaker than the Christ in the word of his brother; his own heart is uncertain, his brother's is sure.[7]

Bonhoeffer reminds us that God designed his people to be *interdependent*, needing to rely on one another for life and growth in Christ. In rehearsing the gospel in word and deed to one another, we encourage one another to maintain the faith until the end (Heb. 10:24–25).

In consideration of Bonhoeffer's words about our need to hear the gospel on the lips of another, we acknowledge the need for companionship is as real and pressing for pastors as it is for members. As pastors ourselves, we can attest to our own dependence on other Christians to endure in our faith and our calling to ministry. This is why we emphasize that the greatest benefit of multichurch models is collaboration. They provide the opportunity to colabor for the gospel with other pastors. The result of such joyful collaboration is not only the church's fruitfulness but one another's health as well. Such well-being cannot be overvalued. The great lie pastors often believe is that the office they hold makes them unable to be human beings with needs, emotions, and crises. Often, the church reinforces this idea and expects its leaders to carry the weight of the church, with all its failures and struggles, without a wince or complaint or a need for help. But there is a better way. As the African proverb underscores, "If you want to go fast, go alone. If you want to go far, go together."

Ephesians 4 affirms that Christ has given gifted leaders to his body whose task is to equip the church's participating members for the work of ministry. Such collaboration is essential for the maturity and multiplication of the church. It is a collaboration of the head with the body, and each part of the body with the other parts. Collaboration between Christ and the church removes the burden of sheer human effort that can never effect what is required, namely, supernatural growth and expansion. Collaboration among church leaders lightens the governance load and diversifies perspectives, ideas, and approaches to ministry. Collaboration among church members eases the ministry load and employs resourceful people in roles they are well-equipped to do. Indeed, "from him [Christ, the head] the whole body, joined and held together by every supporting ligament, grows and builds itself up in love, as each part does its work" (v. 16). What a picture! The whole body, with all its diverse parts working, is linked and bound together, collaborating fully as it extends and deepens itself in love through the grace of Christ. Importantly, the methodology and structure of multichurch models is built on this vision of unity and collaboration toward this magnificent goal.

Environments Thrive Through Diversity

Returning to the theme of unity in Ephesians 4, we should recall that the goal is *not* being identical, achieving sameness or standardization. Unity is being made one, as different parts are combined or ordered to promote a whole. So while uniformity rejects diversity and is destroyed by it, unity embraces diversity and flourishes because of it. The church is one, but its oneness does not mean the members lose their individual identity. On the contrary, the distinctiveness of the members, and the diversity of gifts and roles, is crucial to the church's health and expansion. The church requires members with complementary gifts and ministries united for the well-being of the whole. Such diversity should be celebrated and cultivated.

God has given us examples of the beauty of unity with diversity in nature. When scientists assess the health of an ecosystem, they measure its biodiversity, which is the variety of life in a particular habitat. Measuring biodiversity is a means of gauging the quality and quantity of different organisms that exist within an ecosystem. What scientists find is that the more biodiversity within the ecosystem, the healthier the habitat, and the more likely it is to be sustainable. Another example is the importance of genetic diversity in human procreation. We know that lack of genetic diversity leads to genetic mutation, often resulting in physical, social, and mental impairment. For this reason we have rules about whom we can and cannot marry. Nature itself confirms the importance of unity with diversity.

To borrow from the genetics example above, what should we think about church leaders who insist on controlling the DNA of their church? The motive for control in these cases seems to be a concern for uniformity, not a vision of unity that embraces diversity. One of the potential conse-quences of focusing on DNA control is that the church marginalizes the diverse people, gifts, and ideas that God intends to use for the church's maturity and multiplication. Restricting such diverse influences may leave the church with "genetic mutations" and render it unable to survive in a changing habitat.

In contrast, God has designed the church to be a united body made up of diverse people and gifts. Its leaders are diverse: apostles, prophets, evangelists, pastors and teachers. The consistent New Testament model of church leadership is a plurality of elders, not a solo pastor (e.g., Acts 14:23; 1 Tim. 5:17). Church members are also diverse, being different parts of the one whole. And all this amazing diversity is fueled by the triune God: "There are different kinds of gifts, but the same Spirit distributes them. There are different kinds of service, but the same Lord. There are different kinds of working, but in all of them and in everyone it is the same God at work" (1 Cor. 12:4–6). So there is a plurality and diversity of leaders, members, gifts, and ministries. Churches ought to resist the error of the Corinthian congregation, with some of its members claiming "I follow Paul," others asserting "I follow Apollos," others maintaining "I follow Cephas [Peter]," and still others alleging "I follow Christ" (1 Cor. 1:12). It is both strange and wrong that churches tend to rally around one gifted leader. Rather, churches should strive for unity with diversity, with a plurality of leaders aiding this goal.

Certainly it is true that pillar model churches can develop unity, diversity, and leadership plurality. However, we are excited about the multichurch model because it has those realities built into its structure from the start. Critics who decry the cult of personality in the multichurch model should proceed circumspectly, because that same charge can fall on their churches if diversity and plurality are not cultivated. That is where we believe the multichurch model has an advantage. It has inherent qualities that enable it to combat such dangers by broadening and developing the church's leadership. Driven by conviction, the multichurch model builds structures that provide rich opportunities for diverse people with distinct gifts to participate in the ministry and leadership of those churches. Indeed, the development of both cooperative and collective multichurches require a much larger pool of leaders—pastors, staff, and volunteers—than even large pillar model churches possess. A larger leadership pool means more diversity, and when such diversity bonds in unity, healthier expressions of the church multiply.

Cultivating unity in diversity and broadening leadership has another advantage: together they lead to unique expressions of the church to address the surrounding culture. This phenomenon is encouraged through the addition of voices that know both the church and the surrounding culture and help the church to adapt its expression so as to challenge and shape the culture. Advocates for multisite have always celebrated this type of contextualization.[8] Unfortunately, many multisite models tend to import or to export culture, rather than contextualizing it. The gallery model, for example, imports several cultures into one location. By exaggerating distinctions through multiple diverse services or through various venues that offer different worship experiences, this model fails to contextualize the gospel to the culture around it. Additionally, the model struggles to bring unity to the diversity within its congregation. Conversely, due to heavy centralization, the franchise and some federation models tend to have the opposite problem—exporting one uniform culture. Control over the church's brand leads to the exportation of a standardized culture. Our point is that various multisite models import or export cultures to differing degrees; thus, they all struggle to contextualize.

The apostle Paul's evangelistic boast—"I have become all things to all people so that by all possible means I might save some" (1 Cor. 9:22)— stands in opposition to the importing and exporting of a stereotyped Christian culture. Paul explains the reason for his contextualization: "I do all this for the sake of the gospel, that I may share in its blessings" (1 Cor. 9:23). The gospel is the message of a particular member of the Trinity (the second person, the Son) whom the Father sent on a particular mission (to become incarnate) as Jesus of Nazareth. This particular God-man was "born of a woman [the particular Virgin Mary], born under the law [the particular law of Moses], to redeem those under the law [a particular people], that we might receive adoption to sonship [a particular mighty work of God]" (Gal. 4:4–5). This particular gospel intersects with particular people, who are located in space, time, body, and culture. Their ability to hear and understand the good news is wrapped up in their particular story, which cannot be separated from these particularities. In order to spread this good news, the church must be able to contextualize the gospel into the space, time, embodiment, and culture of future brothers and sisters, even as Paul did. Multichurch models cultivate such contextualization by broadening the leadership of the church, providing more opportunities for different voices to connect with the culture, and fostering unity with diversity. This in turn helps combat the rampant, yet widely ignored, reductionism in the church, which we will look at next.

Avoiding Reductionism

Here's an unavoidable fact: churches reflect the strengths and weaknesses of their lead pastor. This should not be a surprise. People go where they are led, and they become like the ones they follow. A lead pastor who loves evangelism but eschews counseling should not be shocked to find himself leading a hospitable, seeker-friendly church with a nonexistent or weaker than average care ministry. Similarly, a lead pastor who is passionate about theology but avoids relationships should not be dismayed to find himself shepherding a doctrinally sound, formal church with a nonexistent or weaker than average community life. This is the natural development of the church as members follow their leader and reflect his passions and insecurities.

Couple this fact with the recent trend of calling churches to simplify, and these tendencies become even more pronounced. The call to simplify has been co-opted from several business-oriented books like *Good to Great* and *Simplify*.[9] Starting with this emphasis, churches have been challenged to be more selective regarding the ministries and activities to which they commit themselves. We believe the challenge to focus on the things churches have traditionally done well is sound advice. Minimally, it improves the odds of excelling in a few key areas rather than being mediocre in many.[10]

But there is a hidden danger in this momentum—the danger of reductionism.

When a church (leaning toward the preferences of its leader) starts eliminating ministries it sees as peripheral while reinvesting in its strengths, the first phenomenon—the leader's passion—ends up being magnified. The result is a simple and effective church that is inherently limited in scope and tied closely to the strengths of its leader. For many this outcome may be well and good. However, a problem arises if an irreducible complexity to the church is mandated, or at least expected, by God in his Word. In such a case the church cannot simply design itself to be efficient. Rather, it must consider the intent and will of its Lord. We are often amazed at God's capacity to employ inefficient, and what seems to be overly complex, means to accomplish his redemptive plans! Is it possible that the ends to which God aims *use*, or even *demand*, such inefficiency and complexity? If this is the case, our churches may not only be efficient but deficient as well. This is what we call *ecclesiological reductionism*.

This reductionism can take several forms. We see this manifested theologically when a church oversimplifies the good news of the gospel for the sake of clarity, unwittingly stripping it of its inexhaustible mystery, power, and depth. We see this reductionism demonstrated philosophically when a church shrinks the scope of its vision to glorifying God *or* promoting the growth of Christians *or* engaging in the fulfillment of the Great Commission, thereby letting go of several truths that must be held together.

If complexity is expected and even necessary in the design and formation of a church, then it is incumbent upon us to ask two questions: First, what are the irreducible complexities that should characterize the church? Second, how can we build a church that holds these complexities in tension? In keeping with our purpose in this book, we will focus our attention on the second question: specifically, how do multichurch models promote a more robust expression of the church? Ecclesiological reductionism thrives in the presence of uniformity, standardization, and control—especially when the lead pastor promotes them in order to push his strengths and preferences. Consequently, church members and ministries that do not align with the gifts and passions of the lead pastor often get ignored or dismissed. This move toward limitation in turn reduces the opportunity for the church as a whole to grow in maturity and health. As we have seen, ways to combat this reductionism include promoting contextualization by broadening the leadership of the church, providing more opportunities for different voices to be heard, and fostering unity with a diversity of gifts and passions. Multichurch pushes against and overcomes this ecclesiological reductionism.

Multichurch models still feature churches that reflect their leaders, but there is also an intentional effort to seek unity as the diverse congregations come together as one church. In this one whole, diversity and complexity abound. Each congregation manifests unique gifts and commitments, which when joined together contribute to the church as a whole. One congregation may feature mercy ministry and pastoral care. Another may excel at children's ministry and discipleship through community groups. Still another may have strengths in missions and education. As these churches unite as one church, all these gifts and passions characterize the whole. As we have seen in Ephesians 4, this flourishing of unity in diversity represents God's design for the church. Multichurch models foster this vision of the body of Jesus Christ in a way that goes beyond being another acceptable form. In some contexts they should be the preferred models, as they are uniquely designed to combat ecclesiological reductionism and foster multiplication.

Driving Multiplication

Ephesians 4 envisions the church as a unified body of diverse people and gifts working together to fulfill the mission of God, and this is a theme coursing through Paul's letter. The mystery of God's will, which he purposed in Christ, is "to bring unity to all things in heaven and on earth under Christ" (Eph. 1:10). Such unity—which overcomes the key problem in Paul's context, the separation between Jews and Gentiles—is actualized by Christ, whose "purpose was to create in himself one new humanity out of the two, thus making peace, and in one body to reconcile both of them to God through the cross, by which he put to death their hostility" (Eph. 2:15–16). The message of this reconciliation was entrusted to the apostle Paul, whose ministry was

> to preach to the Gentiles the boundless riches of Christ, and to make plain to everyone the administration of this mystery, which for ages past was kept hidden in God, who created all things. His intent was

that now, through the church, the manifold wisdom of God should be made known to the rulers and authorities in the heavenly realms, according to his eternal purpose that he accomplished in Christ Jesus our Lord. (Eph. 3:8–11)

As Sinclair Ferguson summarizes,

> The church lies at the very center of the eternal purpose of God. It is not a divine afterthought. It is not an accident of history. On the contrary, the church is God's new community. For His purpose, conceived in a past eternity, being worked out in history, and to be perfected in a future eternity, is not just to save isolated individuals and so perpetuate our loneliness but rather to build His church, that is, to call out of the world a people for His own glory.[11]

This statement sums up the mission of God and emphasizes both an internal dynamic (growth, maturity) and an external activity (contextualization, multiplication). The mission is actualized through the church's gifted leaders and ministry-engaged members. Jesus did not just give only shepherds and teachers. He also gave apostles, prophets, and evangelists. Through the Holy Spirit, he gives a wide diversity of gifts—at least one to each Christian (1 Cor. 12:7, 11)—which all the members, equipped by the leaders, employ for ministry. Therefore, the goal for the church and its structures is to promote the multiplication of the church.

Multichurch structures are built for this very purpose: multiplication. In the cooperative model, multiple interdependent churches come together as one. In the collective model, a collection of independent churches collaborate as one church. The resources—gifted leaders and members with a wide diversity of gifts—are astounding, and they contribute to the growth of the church. For both models, the churches themselves are tangible testimonies to the focus on multiplication, as each is an expansion of the one church into new contexts. Moreover, the commitment to the multiplication of new churches is always a top priority. This multichurch value can be readily realized by harnessing its passion for starting new communities (e.g., discipleship groups), launching new connected churches (collaborating as the one church), and planting new autonomous churches (not part of the one church). This unifying vision helps church members understand and participate in multiplication. Indeed, the emphasis on multiplication constantly reminds members of the joyful opportunity they have to spread the gospel, which can be a much needed encouragement in the midst of the personal losses that expansion always requires.

The multichurch framework of multiplication, as it structures the organization, also leads to a replication of leaders. Indeed, the multichurch model provides significantly more opportunities for members to lead and to use their gifts for the extension of the church. In part, this is due to the additional roles that multichurch models require of their members, as well as the additional responsibilities that are given to members through expansion at the fringes of the organization. This demand for leaders provides a fertile ground for training the next generation of ministers, missionaries, and church planters.

Conclusion

On the basis of Ephesians 4:1–16 and its presentation of God's goal for the church, we have looked at seven implications for the church's structures and methodologies: unity in the body of Christ, unity versus uniformity, presence and proximity, collaboration, diversity and thriving, overcoming ecclesiological reductionism, and multiplication. Our conviction is that multichurch models promote these seven elements, often better than other models of the church. In saying this we are not suggesting that a multichurch model is the ideal paradigm in every situation. But if a church finds itself in a situation where it has a growing congregation, and it desires an approach that promotes unity, diversity, collaboration, and expansion (rather than reductionism) while providing a solid framework for maturity and multiplication, we believe that a multichurch model is the best solution. This is why multichurch is the future of multisite.

Join the evolution!

ORIENTEERING

Good planning is important. I've also regarded a sense of humor as one of the most important things on a big expedition. When you're in a difficult or dangerous situation, or when you're depressed about the chances of success, someone who can make you laugh eases the tension.

SIR EDMUND HILLARY

Orienteering is a fancy term for land navigation. It involves using maps to develop a plan to navigate the terrain ahead. In the first section we spent some time getting the lay of the land and identifying landmarks and landmines. Now it is time to plot a course forward. In this section we will break down the steps to developing a healthy multichurch, specifically looking at five critical areas that need to be reenvisioned for your church to move into the future with confidence. We will examine the organization as a whole and specifically its polity, ministry, finances, and membership. We will also lay out concepts and give you some practical exercises you can do to help you prepare for the adventure of becoming a multichurch.

6

MultiOrg

Up to this point, we have talked about the multichurch model in the abstract, as an idea based on principles of authority and power. But what does it look like in practice? What does it mean to have one church with many congregations, or one church made up of multiple churches? Getting your head around it can be overwhelming.

This chapter sets forth the process and principles that can help guide the transition into multichurch and help you organize the church so that it flourishes. As we elaborate upon these organization principles, we want to avoid the mistake of separating the organization of the church from the biblical and theological convictions we laid out earlier. As we recounted earlier, the impetus for our church, Sojourn Community Church, to transition to a multichurch model came from experiencing the deficiencies of a federation multisite model without enjoying the benefits. This led to a fair amount of frustration and, eventually, a complete reevaluation of Sojourn's organization. In this process we made a very important discovery: our experience of the church and its structure did not align with our biblical convictions. This disconnect drove us to rethink our methodology, and in doing so, we talked to several other churches to better understand the different options available within the multisite movement.

This book is the fruit of that painful reevaluation process and is where we originally developed the taxonomy we created for this book—including the distinction between multisite models and multichurch models. It also led to a distillation of our convictions regarding these two broad categories of churches. As is often the case, friction and frustration provided an opportunity for refinement that has culminated in a much healthier organization.

As we refined our biblical and theological convictions about the nature and function of the church, we converged on three maxims to guide us in organization:

1. Multichurch exists for its churches.
2. Everything cannot matter.
3. Multiplication is nonnegotiable.

These are the three maxims of multichurch, and in what follows we will show how each of these maxims influences multichurch organization.

Maxim #1:
Multichurch Exists for Its Churches

The one church that is made up of multiple interdependent churches (cooperative model) or that links multiple independent churches (collective model) exists for its component churches and not the other way around. When a church has developed from a central authority structure, recognizing this can be a humbling discovery for the church and its leadership. It may seem obvious, but it may not be true of the systems and structures of the church. In fact, the very opposite might be true. In many cases the church's central operations dominate the vision, finances, energy, training, and concern of the organization. Indeed, our experience and research indicate this may be the most significant maxim in resetting a church's trajectory.

Kingdoms and Empires

Building a multichurch that exists for its churches begins with understanding what type of ecosystem you are building. Lyle Wells, of the Flippen Group, has observed that most churches fall into one of two categories: kingdoms or empires.[1]

Empires are built for the benefit of their leader or leaders. Emperors tax some citizens, enslave others, and expand without empathy for the sake of self-glorification. Jim Collins calls this "the undisciplined pursuit of more."[2]

Kingdoms in contrast are built for the benefit of their citizens. In healthy kingdoms the monarchs see their calling as an opportunity to serve their people. In multichurch language, they exist for the local church.

One of the reasons that multisite models are legitimately criticized is their tendency to become empires. Success is a seductress. Platform building, book writing, and getting mentioned on fastest growing churches lists become more important than quietly and faithfully making disciples. Churches might decide to grow in order to increase the reach of the empire and craft their communication to sell it as mission.

A multisite church's vision cannot evolve unless the leadership commits to building a kingdom and embraces the maxim of existing for its local churches. If it does not seek this, it will likely succumb to one of two (or both) stumbling blocks that trip up most multisite churches: self-preservation and self-justification. When this happens, multisite churches begin to operate as though each contextualized location or local church exists to preserve and support the whole, leading to a loss of ownership and organizational decline. When developing the organization of a multichurch, it is important to understand these two dangers and respond accordingly.

The Falsehood of Self-Preservation

Thankfully, few of us have ever been in a survival situation that put us face-to-face with the reality of possible death. When we are in a situation like that, our natural instinct is self-preservation. This is sometimes called the "first law of nature" because all living organisms, when endangered, exhibit this reflex. The threat of death causes a physiological response intended to keep us alive. In the case of extreme cold, for example, our body begins to limit the blood flow to our limbs in order to preserve heat and force blood into our core. Our body reacts this way because we can live without our toes but not without our heart. In survival mode, our body naturally sacrifices our extremities to preserve our existence.

The organization of a church follows a similar pattern. The threat of decline or death instinctively drives the church to build systems to preserve the core. This is seen as a "natural" way to ensure organizational self-preservation. The church may not even know it is in survival mode. Sadly, these natural reactions can end up having the opposite effect. Instead of helping the church to survive and grow, they end up delaying death. They stifle growth, foster disenchantment, provoke anger and bitterness, and sometimes lead to apathy among leaders and members. When the church preserves its existence, it is not promoting life. Mere existence is not the goal; we want churches that thrive.

Why does this happen? Self-preservation is based on the faulty premise that the church's central structure is the source of its life. It is why leaders focus their efforts there when things seem to be dying. They see the center as the most important aspect to be maintained. However, God's economy doesn't operate that way; it turns this assumption on its head. Our savior died so that we might live, and self-preservation, though a real option for Jesus—"My Father, if it is possible, may this cup be taken from me"—was not the choice he made—"Yet not as I will, but as you will" (Matt. 26:39). He resisted the natural instinct for self-preservation. Instead, he chose self-sacrifice so that we might live. Similarly, the church cannot thrive and multiply with a mentality of self-preservation; it needs a spirit of self-sacrifice. The church does not exist for itself, but for others.

Therefore, the church's central structure is not its source of life. The lifeblood of the church, the place where self-sacrifice for others happens, is in the trenches—in the contextualized locations or the local churches. That's where God is worshiped. That's where members are discipled. That's where unbelievers embrace the gospel. That's where care is expressed. That's where mercy meets needs. These miracles happen in churches and in members' homes. So if we want to preserve the church and enable it to grow and thrive, resourcing these places is paramount. The one church—specifically its central organization and leadership—exists to encourage and support the contextualized locations and the particular churches, ensuring they are maturing and multiplying.

The Problem of Self-Justification

Related to the falsehood of self-preservation, but often far more insidious, is the problem of self-justification. This is the compulsion to vindicate our existence. The organization spends vast amounts of time and energy offering reasons or rationalizations in an attempt to convince itself and others its decisions and actions are good and right. Self-justification often entails a department or a team puffing itself up to appear more important or indispensable to the organization than it really is.

My first exposure to this type of self-justification was when I (Brad) was a child and my dad attempted to explain the economics of state budgeting. He was the overseer of a large department within the state organization and was responsible for developing a budget and managing its distribution in various projects. This required that he travel around the state to listen to and present proposals on how to spend departmental money. After one such trip he expressed frustration with the value of the project he had presented that day. As it was rare for my dad to complain about work, his story piqued my interest. His frustration stemmed from the fact that the project was not in the least bit necessary. Being a precocious preteen, I counseled my troubled father to simply reject the project and save the money for next year. Here is where I learned my first lesson on how the government works—a lesson in the hard truth of self-justification. My dad informed me that my solution would not work. If his department did not spend their allocated money during the current fiscal year, next year's budget would be cut. If that happened, there would be inadequate money to fund projects that actually need funding. Practically, this meant that his department had to spend money now to justify its existence.

Sadly, this is not just a problem in our government bureaucracy. Self-justification in the church works in much the same way. Small departments are often seen as less essential—if they were important, then they would obviously need more money and a bigger staff. This type of thinking drives those departments to find reasons to increase the number of staff and augment their budget in order to prove their importance to the church. Of course, this type of rationalization leads to bloated staffs and the inefficient use of funds. This is precisely the mechanism that inflates the central staff and central budget of many churches. However, the first maxim—multichurch exists for its churches—keeps such inflation in check and promotes the efficient use of staff and funds.

Our ability to lead in this way without the need to justify our existence comes from our identity in Christ. As we said before, the gospel should be just as apparent within the organization of the church as it is within the lives of its people. As our identity in Christ impacts our organizational philosophy and structure, it frees us from leading out of fear. Such confidence allows us to make decisions and act without the impulse toward self-justification. If our department or staff position is no longer essential for the mission of the church, then we don't seek to preserve it. The ability to make decisions and act without self-justification is essential for a church to be able to adapt to the challenges of a complex and growing organization.

Understanding the Organizational Lifecycle

The devastating effects of self-preservation and self-justification become clear when we look at the lifecycle of an organization. The diagram that follows, adapted from several sources on organizational theory, traces the typical lifecycle of a church.[3]

Every organization follows the same basic lifecycle, churches included. In the early stages of a church plant, the lead pastor and his launch team are driven by vision, outreach, and creativity. The organizational structure supports ministry and mission. Self-preservation and self-justification are blips on the radar screen. As the church matures and grows, new influences (the need to support staff and their families, the voice of tradition, the reach for control, and the desire to maintain success) enter and exert pressure. When decline sets in, the church longs for "the good old days," becomes rigid and apathetic with low morale, orients itself toward problem-solving, and focuses on survival. Self-preservation rears its ugly head. The church seeks to preserve its existence but does not promote life. Self-justification takes over, with staff and ministries seeking to rationalize their existence, leading to conflict and division.

Organizational Lifecycle

MATURITY

Effective Ministry

Opportunity
Evangelism (Reach)
Growth
Sacrifice
Cooperation
Disciple-Making (Build)

Structure

Serves Ministry
Leads to the Future
Adances the Mission

MAINTENANCE

Plateau/Lost Vision

Safety
Inward Focus
Control
Tradition
Maintenance
Desires Guarantee

Apathy

Rigid
Changeless
Complex
Looks to the Past

GROWTH

Goals

Growth
Creativity
Reach, Build, Release

Beliefs

Values
Mission

DECLINE

Questioning

Problem Oriented
Survival Oriented
Low Morale
Doubt
Think as Individuals

Beliefs

Division
Intense Conflict

BIRTH

Dream

Vision

DEATH

Implosion

People Leave

This organizational lifecycle mirrors human existence from birth to death, and it harmonizes nicely with our understanding of the church as a living organism. Like all organisms, decline and death are inevitable. Still, this demise can be delayed and, in some ways, held at bay indefinitely. As humans, we delay our demise by attending to our health and seeking to extend our productive years, and we seek to hold death at bay in the long term by establishing a legacy through our children. As a church, both means are available to extend its existence and impact: the church strives for constant renewal of its health through innovative steps toward maturity, and it expands its legacy of fruitful ministry through concerted efforts toward multiplication.

Where is your church on the lifecycle curve? Objectively, you can look at various metrics to determine your church's location in the lifecycle. Subjectively, however, your perspective can make it difficult to assess where the entire organization fits on the curve. For example, you evaluate your church's governance and policies, and determine that your church is at the front end of maturity. As you assess your church's growth numbers—such as attendance, community group participation, and giving—you conclude that the church is in the growth phase. All these metrics seem to indicate a healthy church.

But looks can be deceiving. In the case of organizational maturity, the establishment of sound leadership and policies may have come later in your church's life, with its governance and management practices lagging behind the church's actual lifecycle. As for growth numbers, these are the hardest markers to use for assessment because an organization, even when in decline, can still produce results due to the momentum of earlier growth. Many companies and churches continue to achieve good outcomes when deep into decline, only to realize the danger when it is too late. Knowing this fact, we must consider which markers are the best for assessing the church's health. These markers are the attitudes, behaviors, and morale of the staff and volunteers. They are indicated in the boxes on the lifestyle curve above. These markers can help you evaluate where your church is on the lifecycle and determine its trajectory. As the curve shows, the devastating effects of self-preservation and self-justification—reduction of vision, pining for "the good old days," lack of passion to reach unbelievers, rigidity, control, apathy, low morale, doubt, conflict, and survival mode—locate a church in the range from maintenance to decline.

We are not saying that the staff and volunteers are at fault for the church's decline. In fact, decline is part of the natural arc of an organization and is, in some ways, enhanced by the complexity of large multisite churches. A multisite church can create a culture in which its leaders and staff operate apart from the church's vision. Such developments are dangerous. It is incumbent upon the leadership to direct and inspire the staff to accomplish the mission God has for the church. The good news is that by identifying this phenomenon early, the leaders can make changes that will breathe new life into the church and initiate a new growth phase with the Spirit's provision.

The beauty of multichurch models is the constant renewal of life that is fueled by the addition of new churches and their leaders. This revitalization stimulates the multichurch's leadership to remain humble, inspires its membership to participate faithfully in ministry, and prompts its organization to stay nimble, in order that the church may continue to mature and multiply as it adapts to the movement of God within its city.

The Benefits of Ownership

If there is a fountain of youth for organizations, it is ownership. Negatively, this means that a decline in an organization is often paralleled by a decline in ownership. What is ownership? In a church, ownership is about possessing the vision; embracing the identities, doctrine, and values; and supporting the ministries of the church. Such ownership should not be limited to a select few, such as the church's leaders, but must be the possession of each and every member. The members are the "stakeholders" and partners in the mission, and the level of "buy in" correlates with the commitment of the church's nonleaders. This is why the indicators of ownership—attitudes, behaviors, and morale—of the staff and volunteers make the best markers for evaluating the life-stage of a church.

Brad writes extensively on the importance of ownership for the health and mission of the church in his book *Community: Taking Your Small Group Off Life Support.* He shares this example of what we mean when we talk about ownership:

> My wife and I have owned two homes in our life. The first thing we do when we buy a home is paint. And just to be clear, when I say "we" paint, I generally mean that she picks out the colors and I paint. This ritual is a way for us to make the house our own. There is no law that makes us paint the house or take care of it. Rather, this is our response to ownership. Because I own it, it's my responsibility to maintain it and improve it toward some semblance of its intended glory.
>
> In contrast, I have never painted an apartment. It is not mine. When something breaks, it is the landlord's responsibility to fix it. This is a picture of many of our churches today. Leaders have become landlords of a rented mission.
>
> I have observed, even in the most articulate and missional churches, a disparity in ownership of the mission between the leadership of the church and the church itself. While leaders of the church may be passionate and driven toward the goals set out by their mission, they often face a congregation that is passive or even apathetic. The church lacks ownership. They have not internalized the mission to the point of it becoming their own. You could say that they haven't painted the walls.
>
> If we want to accomplish the mission of the church, then we need to get brushes in every hand. We need to make sure that ownership does not reside only in the elders and pastors of the church, but is instead shared by every member.[4]

Ownership matters, which is why we see the multichurch model as a positive development. Multichurch stimulates a high degree of ownership in everyone from the founder(s) of the church, to its present leaders, to the church staff, and to the members who serve in various ministries. We have found great difficulty in engendering ownership in multisite models that feature a strong central authority and only secondarily have campuses or sites that express the central church. In such multisite churches, there is always a landlord divesting the people of ownership. This is even more evident when the campuses or sites exist primarily for the purpose of maintaining that entity.

By contrast, multichurch models promote the full participation of each congregation and teach that each and every member of the church has a part to play in its health and mission. That is, each part is indispensable to the whole (1 Cor. 12:12–27) and contributes to its flourishing (Eph. 4:1–16). Ownership permeates the entire organization, especially at the local level, by empowering every member to use their gifts for ministry. Correspondingly, organizational structures must be built to push decision making to the edges of the church.[5] Participation in the mission of the church breeds ownership, which in turn helps to maintain the church's freshness, fuels ongoing renewal, and delays decay. And where there is whole-body ownership, the church yields much fruit.

Feed the Fruit

Any gardener knows the secret to cultivating plants that produce bountiful fruit: ensure that the plants—and specifically the branches that are producing fruit—get all the water and nutrients they need. When these resources are in limited supply, the gardener arranges the garden and prunes the plants to prevent waste. Jesus, speaking of his Father as a gardener, declares, "He cuts off every branch in me that bears no fruit, while every branch that does bear fruit he prunes, so that it will be even more fruitful" (John 15:2). Transposing this agricultural principle for the church, a simple syllogism emerges: (1) if the fruit of the church is participation in the mission of God, and (2) if participation is a product of ownership, then (3) multichurch models should give as many resources to the local churches as possible, in order to encourage ownership and foster God-given growth.

This discussion underscores our first maxim: *multichurch exists for its churches.* The implications of this concept should be felt throughout the organization. As we will see in the following chapters, this maxim affects the polity, ministry, finances, and membership of a multichurch.

Maxim #2:
Everything Cannot Matter

Our second maxim is that everything cannot matter. To qualify this maxim, everything cannot matter at least to the extent that it is critical to the organization's viability. Leading an organization with the idea that everything is critical leaves the organization in a perpetual state of crisis that will lead to burnout or disengagement.

As a multisite church, Sojourn learned this maxim in a humiliating way—as we seem to learn all our lessons. While visiting a church that employs a multichurch model, we explored some of their methods and noticed that they seemed to be at odds with our own. This would not have been a big deal except that we felt we had explored all other models, and frankly, we were surprised to see their systems working so well. This led us to be defensive, and we tried to find holes in their model. We asked them some aggressive questions like "How do you do this?" and "Why does that work?" We kept running into an impenetrable wall, a single question they repeated back to us with every question we asked them: *Why does that matter to you?* They found our kryptonite. For us, *everything* seemed to matter.

Leaders of large, growing organizations usually achieve their success by caring about the details that make their organization flourish. But leaders cannot care about everything. They are limited in terms of what they can give their attention to, and there are many things that demand their attention. Good leadership relinquishes control in order to foster collective ownership, thereby spreading out the care for the organization among several people.

A key organizational principle in business, called the founder's dilemma, expresses the idea this way: "Founders who want to manage empires will not believe they are successes if they lose control, even if they end up rich. Conversely, founders who understand that their goal is to amass wealth will not view themselves as failures when they step down from the top job."[6] In other words, do you want to be rich or be king? At some point, business entrepreneurs need to decide whether they want to make a lot of money or if they want to remain in control. You cannot have both.[7]

This truism can easily be applied to ministry if we define success as kingdom advancement. Nothing will stunt the growth of an organization like the belief that everything matters, combined with the idea that only a select group of people—its leaders—bear all the responsibility for the organization's success. Humility is key. Leaders need to relinquish control, foster a sense of ownership in others, encourage others to work toward and receive credit for the organization's success, and empower them for more. This process cannot be done if everything is critical.

To think that everything matters also presents leaders with a practical conundrum. If something truly matters to the church's mission, then the church has a moral obligation, if at all possible, to invest in that mission. A church where everything matters becomes buried by the obligation to invest in everything. An example we worked through at Sojourn was the Sunday bulletin. It might seem innocuous enough, but our church places a high value on aesthetics and the arts. In Sojourn's early years, the bulletin was a regular opportunity to display that value. Each week the bulletin incorporated original art work, but producing art on a weekly schedule was no easy task—especially when working with artists! Printing the bulletin in the central office and transporting those copies to four locations was also difficult, and difficult tasks require many resources. Could the bulletin continue to matter—along with everything else? As Sojourn considered making a transition to a multichurch model, the necessary step of redistributing resources to its four churches meant it needed to care less about the bulletin. And so the decision was made to decentralize bulletin production. Each church would design and print the bulletin for itself, even if that meant the bulletin would no longer display original art work. While Sojourn continues to highly value the arts, the church had to let go of one of its artistic expressions. Everything cannot matter.

Unfortunately, not every decision will be as easy as dealing with the bulletin. The transition into a multichurch model requires a church to rethink its priorities and decide what matters, how much it matters, and when it matters. These three distinct yet related ideas about priorities must be sorted out.

What Matters?

The maxim that everything cannot matter should not be misunderstood to mean that nothing matters. All-or-nothing leaders will have to work hard not to flip this switch. Rather, the maxim that everything cannot matter is about the prioritization of values. The process of deciding what matters to a church is analogous to zero-based budgeting. Zero-based budgeting requires that all expenses be justified at the beginning of each fiscal year. The budget restarts at zero every year, then is rebuilt. From a value standpoint, this prioritization process entails a regular evaluation of what has come to be considered nonnegotiable, in order to determine if that really is the case. Does it matter?

How Much Does It Matter?

If it does matter, the next question is how much does it matter? Things that matter are priorities, but not everything can be a top priority. If everything is most important, then nothing actually is. Zero-based prioritization entails assigning a value to each thing that matters. There are several ways to do this. One way is to chart priorities based on conviction versus urgency.[8]

Urgency is a measure of how critical a particular ministry, issue, value, or program is to the success of a church's mission. For a church with a growing number of families, updating the kids' space may be a more urgent issue than upgrading the music quality. When a church becomes involved in a crisis—a flood destroying much of the neighborhood or an influx of immigrants into the city—supporting mercy ministries may be more urgent than putting money into savings. Keep in mind that urgency is not the same as conviction. If a church's highest conviction is theological orthodoxy, but the sense is positive about doctrinal orthodoxy among its churches and leaders, theological orthodoxy will be high in conviction but low in urgency.

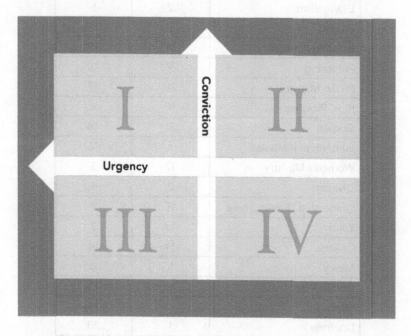

If you want to see how this conviction-urgency chart works in your own church, stop and take twenty minutes to list your church's top twenty issues or concerns. For example:

Evangelism	International Mission	Community
Prayer	Women's Ministry	Music
Building Addition	Diversity	Doctrine
Preaching	Leadership Development	Parking
Prison Ministry	Youth	Arts
Kids' Programs	College	Pastoral Care
Singles	Mercy	

After you have made your list, number it from one to twenty (high to low) in two columns reflecting the sense of conviction you have about each one and then the level of urgency it has.

Issue	Conviction	Urgency
Evangelism	2	5
Prayer	3	1
Building Addition	11	19
Preaching	9	10
Prison Ministry	20	17
Kids' Programs	10	4
Singles	6	18
International Mission	4	16
Women's Ministry	12	3
Diversity	8	9
Leadership Development	19	7
Youth	13	2
College	14	14
Mercy	5	8
Community	16	15
Music	17	11
Doctrine	1	20
Parking	18	6
Arts	15	13
Pastoral Care	7	12

The enumeration ensures that not every issue can be your top issue. Remember the second maxim: everything cannot matter.

Next, place the numbered issues in the quadrants on the chart. For conviction, issues one through ten go above the line, while issues eleven to twenty go below the line. For urgency, issues from one to ten go to the left, while issues from eleven to twenty go to the right. Charting out these twenty issues according to conviction and urgency will give you a sense for what matters most to your church at this moment in time.

The chart has four quadrants, which are now filled with the twenty issues that are a concern for your church.

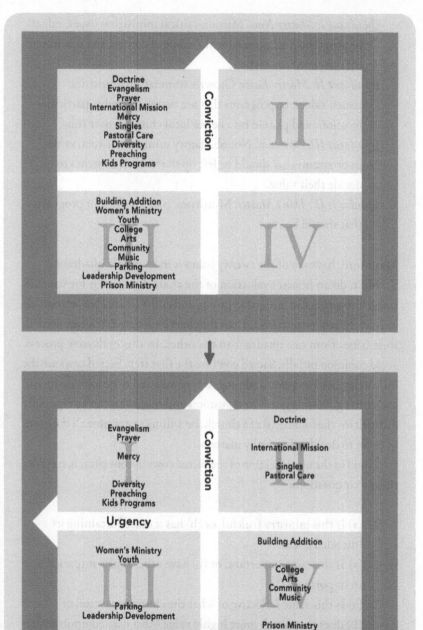

Quadrant I: Matter Now. Mission-critical ministries, issues, values, or programs that determine the scope of control and investment for the church as a whole.

Quadrant II: Matter Later. Growth-stimulating ministries, issues, values, or programs that are better applied at particular locations and phased into newer local churches over time.

Quadrant III: Optional. Nonobligatory ministries, issues, values, or programs that should be left up to the local churches to decide their value.

Quadrant IV: Don't Matter. Ministries, issues, values, or programs that should be cut.

Make sure that each of the twenty issues is in its proper quadrant.

Next, do an honest evaluation of the chart. Examine it for yourself, assess it together as a leadership group, and enlist trusted leaders outside of your church to appraise it. Does the chart look correct? When needed, shift issues from one quadrant to the other. In this evaluative process, avoid common pitfalls. Sacred cows are the first trap. Sacred cows are the ministries, issues, values, and programs considered to be above criticism and cutting. Letting go of these customs and traditions can be especially difficult for the founder(s) of a church. Be willing to examine all the issues in order to decide what really matters.

To aid in the identification of the sacred cows in your church, consider these four questions:

1. (a) Is this ministry fruitful, or (b) has it ceased attaining its intended goals?
2. (a) Is this issue important, or (b) have other topics surpassed it in importance?
3. (a) Is this value reflective of what the church treasures, or (b) does the church more highly value other core commitments?
4. (a) Does this program support the church, or (b) do other structures now bear the program's weight?

If you have predominately (a) answers, then you are most likely not dealing with a sacred cow, and you should continue. If you have predominately (b) answers, then you are most likely dealing with a sacred cow that needs to be put out to pasture.

Additionally, every value-decision is an opportunity either to build ownership within the organization or to diminish it. Look at the issues in the four quadrants and note which ones increase ownership within the church and which ones diminish it, without allowing any of them to be neutral. If the issues in Quadrant I and Quadrant II decrease ownership, the church will struggle to empower its local leaders. Still, some of the issues that decrease ownership are nonnegotiable: they must be high conviction and high urgency. For most high conviction and high urgency issues, the goal is increasing ownership within the church.

With the church's issues charted, the next step is envisioning which ones need to be prioritized (move up to Quadrant I and Quadrant II) and which ones need to receive less attention (move down to Quadrant III and Quadrant IV). Work on plans for making reprioritization a reality—plans that include costs, staff, and control. The conviction-urgency chart and the concrete plans derived from it can help your church to expend resources (i.e., time, money, personnel, and effort) in the most God-honoring and efficient way. As an additional benefit, thinking in terms of urgency and conviction pushes the church's central leadership to empower decision making at the edges—in the local churches.

When Does It Matter?

If it does matter and if it matters much, the next question is *when* does it matter? An issue can matter greatly to an organization without mattering now. When it matters may vary according to the age, size, strength, and calling of the local churches. It may even be crucial for the whole church, but a lack of resources prevents it from mattering right now.

Legacy matters for Sojourn Community Church. It is a high priority for the whole church, because over 20 percent of our weekly attendance is children, most of whom are under the age of twelve. Therefore, we desire to have high-quality kids' spaces at each of our four churches—a dream that reflects our commitment to our future generations. But we have other priorities that compete for a limited pool of resources, making it difficult to build such infrastructures right now. These challenges do not necessitate that we stop caring about kids and our ministries to them. It simply means that we must plan to address these structural needs when we have the opportunity to meet them.

The same can be said for the level of preaching, the quality of music, the aesthetic of worship space, the hospitality of the connect team, the effectiveness of discipleship, and so on. Each issue matters to some degree, but they each take time to develop. We had a hard time letting a two-year-old Sojourn Church be a two-year-old. We wanted it to have highly developed ministries throughout the whole church to match other local churches, and the expectations and demands were stifling. This two-year-old could not keep up because it was still learning to walk. Remember that development is both normal and necessary.

Accordingly, the question of *when* it matters is a function of *how much* an issue matters and the church's *ability* to pull it off. The following conviction-ability chart helps determine when it is time for an issue to matter:

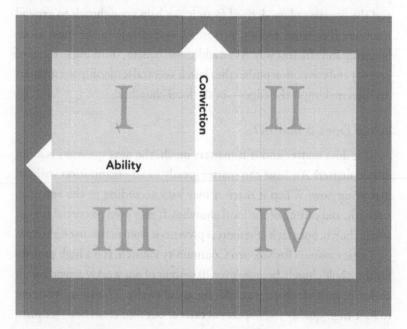

The earlier conviction-urgency chart helped to determine a church's priorities: what matters and how much it matters. As you did with that chart, list your church's top-twenty issues again. The conviction numbers should remain the same, but this time, you are judging your ability to address these issues. Insert the numbers into this new conviction-ability chart. Your church may find that some, perhaps many, issues in Quadrant I and Quadrant II are currently too costly in terms of time, money, personnel, and effort to be implemented church-wide. They should be downgraded on the scale, particularly to Quadrant III, so as to become possible priorities for a local church rather than the whole church.

Taken together, these two charts—the conviction-urgency chart and the conviction-ability chart—can help bring clarity to what really matters to a church. Whatever method or tool you choose, remember that a key to empowerment in multichurch models is the ability to assess what matters, how much it matters, and when it matters.

Maxim #3:
Multiplication Is Nonnegotiable

The third and final maxim guiding multichurch models is that multiplication is nonnegotiable. In 1952, the International Missionary Council in Willingen, Germany stated, "There is no participation in Christ without participation in his mission to the world."[9] This affirmation mirrors Jesus's challenge to his disciples on that first resurrection Sunday: "As the Father has sent me, I am sending you" (John 20:21; cf. Matt. 28:18–20; Luke 24:44–49). In other words, God sent his Son on a mission, and the Son sends his church on that same mission. Far too often the church gets it backwards, thinking that it takes a mission upon itself and can therefore opt to engage in the mission whenever it is convenient. But this approach is completely backwards. As Brad explains in *Community*,

> When this happens, we create a church with a mission. The church
> is the sending agent and the mission is the active outworking of that
> church. Ed Stetzer, a leading missiologist in the church today, argues

that this is a consistent historical mistake of the church. To paraphrase Stetzer, missions should not be a hobby of the church. When we understand the mission of God, we realize that it is the *mission* that has a *church*, not the other way around. God has a mission, to call people to worship and exalt the Son through the work of the Holy Spirit. God is the sending agent and the church is the active outworking of the mission.[10]

It is the mission of God in which the church participates, and that mission defines the identity of the church. It is not optional.

But we are not alone or unequipped for what we are called to do. For this task, Jesus provides the necessary resource. Speaking to his disciples, Jesus promised, "But you will receive power when the Holy Spirit comes on you; and you will be my witnesses in Jerusalem, and in all Judea and Samaria, and to the ends of the earth" (Acts 1:8). The church is to be a witness of Jesus down the block, in the city, around the state, and throughout the world. Multichurch models put Jesus's commission into practice by building multiplicative structures internally and externally.

Jerusalem: Where Mission Begins

The mission starts at home. For multichurch models, this means developing a missional framework throughout the whole church, beginning with launching and multiplying community groups. These missional communities expand the church to reach the whole city. Sojourn's missional motto is "multichurch for city reaching." As we pray for the Spirit to move in our city and empower gospel engagement, we have a mechanism for launching additional interdependent churches in our cooperative model.

All Judea and Samaria: The Next Step in Mission

The inclusion of Judea and Samaria in the mission of the church expanded the vision of the early disciples. The mention of Judea reminded them that the world is bigger than they are. Far beyond this, the mention of Samaria was shocking. The Jews hated the Samaritans and would not even step foot in their land, going so far as to walk completely around it to avoid getting Samaritan dust between their toes. The inclusion of the Samaritans brought the extensiveness of God's plan for reconciliation into full view. The gospel is the good news meant for all people. The church's mission is to spread it everywhere. Accordingly, church planting is not optional. Sojourn as a multichurch launches additional cooperating churches in the Louisville metropolitan area, and as a sending church, we join with others in the Sojourn Network to plant churches throughout the United States.

The Ends of the Earth: God's Global Vision for Mission

Ultimately, Jesus's commission thrusts the gospel around the globe. Certainly, the disciples could not have imagined how far or how quickly this mandate would be accomplished. But in expanding the vision to the ends of the earth, Jesus made it clear that the plan for the church could never be limited to domestic expansion. His gospel has no borders, and the church is called to send out witnesses to the far corners of our planet. By partnering with various agencies (such as the International Mission Board, Pioneers, and Serge), Sojourn engages robustly in international missions.

Threefold Strategy

Developing these three avenues for multiplication takes time but should be a part of the church's vision and long-term plan. By clearly demarcating these three avenues, the church can avoid some common mistakes. One mistake is when churches refer to the start of a new service, or even a new location, as church planting. Recent trends indicate that some multisite churches use this terminology, and it is often accompanied by a decline in sending teams away from the church for church planting. Another error is to refer to launching new churches within a multichurch structure as church planting. While the addition of a new congregation in a multichurch model is rightly called a church, the impulse here is different from that of church planting. The goal of church planting is to send witnesses to places the church cannot physically reach in order to initiate new churches. To summarize the point, to start a new service or new location in a multisite model, to launch a new church as a part of the whole church in a multichurch model, and to plant churches are three different avenues of multiplication. We strongly encourage churches to clarify these distinctions in their plans and keep their funding separate.[11]

Remember the Three Maxims

In this chapter, we have set forth some of the key aspects of how the multichurch model is organized. We proposed and explained three maxims:

1. Multichurch exists for its churches.
2. Everything cannot matter.
3. Multiplication is nonnegotiable.

Additionally, we offered two charts (one that juxtaposes conviction and urgency and another that collocates conviction and ability) and encouraged using them to help churches assess what matters, how much it matters, and when it matters. But there are issues that remain, including the question of leadership and governance in the multichurch model. While multichurch organization is not limited to church leaders, it does involve them primarily. So how should multichurch models be governed? The next chapter presents a redemptive polity that makes this possible.

MultiPolity

The term "polity" is a fancy word for church government. In other words, a church's polity is the way the church is structured for leadership. Historically, there have been three major forms of polity that divide the church of Jesus Christ into episcopal, presbyterian, and congregational governments. While the question of polity is always a matter for consideration, it has become an increasingly important topic for multisite and multichurch models. Why? In recent years there have been some well-publicized leadership failures in some of the largest and most well-known multisite churches. This rash of high-profile pastors resigning or being asked to step down from leadership has raised questions about whether the structure of the church government is partly to blame for this mess.

Considering God's immense love for the church, it may come as a surprise to some that Scripture provides few details on how the church should be governed. Scripture does, however, tell us a fair amount about the character of church leaders. This disparity highlights a key axiom for church government: great character overcomes the weakest polity, and poor character undermines the strongest polity. In either case the character of church leaders trumps the governing structure. Accordingly, this chapter begins with a consideration of what we call *redemptive polity*.

Redemptive Polity

Although establishing leaders of strong character is of the utmost importance, prioritizing character does not make polity irrelevant. While a particular governing philosophy cannot guarantee success or prevent failure, thoughtful polity can provide a measure of protection for both the congregation and its leaders, and provide a careful structure that builds trust while simultaneously freeing leaders to exercise their responsibilities and gifts. These factors of trust and freedom are essential for a living, growing church. Distrust and/or excessive control will choke out maturity and multiplication.

Church governments tend to fall into two extremes. We call the first extreme the "no brakes" polity. To picture this, imagine driving a car with no brakes. You have no need for brakes if you don't intend to stop or change your speed or direction. As long as you are driving straight ahead, everything is fine. It's only when a halt or adjustment becomes necessary that you need brakes—and then you'll really appreciate them!

A "no brakes" polity assumes that church leadership is nearly infallible and has no need for checks and balances. It is born out of an overrealized view of sanctification. This often unstated and untested view assumes that the church and the whole congregation have largely overcome sinfulness and do not need to worry about potential failures among their leaders. This belief leads to a polity structure without a safety net for the church, neither for its leaders nor for its members. To be fair, church plants rarely consider the need for a well-functioning polity—one that will enable them to make the needed adjustments and corrections in the future—especially when they are experiencing growth and expansion. But sooner or later all churches need a good polity.

The second extreme can be just as erroneous. We call it the "parking brake" polity. Imagine a car with its parking brake always engaged. It can never go at full speed, and when it slows down and begins creeping along, if you take your foot off the accelerator, then things grind to a halt. This "parking brake" polity assumes that no one can be trusted. It arises from an underrealized view of sanctification: thinking the church and its people are thoroughly under the dominion of sin and can never be trusted. The polity focuses on the church's fallen condition. This belief results in a government in which every effort is taken to protect the church from its leaders. Designed to thwart failure or abuse, this structure prevents the church from being nimble and gaining the momentum to grow. Such governance is often developed in reaction to the failure of a previous polity or the public failure of other churches. While learning from such disasters is important, reactionary polity is rarely fruitful in the long term. Although it's "safe," the "parking brake" polity inhibits the church from participating fully in the mission of God.

Regardless of their past experience, all churches need a good polity.

Rather than falling into either extreme, churches require a polity that balances these two realities: Christians *have been redeemed* by Jesus, and they *are being redeemed* by him. First, as Christians redeemed by Jesus Christ, we need to remember that we have been made new and are indwelt with the Holy Spirit. What is true of us individually is true of us corporately. Accordingly, our church's polity should expect our leaders to act in godly ways with humility, maturity, and the best interests of our church in mind. A bunch of red tape to prevent abuse is not required. We encourage leaders to walk in faith and to radiate a high level of trust so that unity undergirds the church.

Second, as Christians being redeemed by Jesus Christ, we acknowledge that we are still sinful as we continue to grow in holiness. What is true of us individually is true of us corporately. This means that our church's polity acknowledges the fallen condition of our leaders; therefore, appropriate checks and balances should be put in place. Such a government should include policies that allow leaders to raise concerns about the church or other leaders in a constructive and safe way, while reinforcing trust within the leadership and congregation.

All churches need a good polity: one that expects and requires humility and maturity from the leaders, one that takes seriously ongoing sinfulness and thus holds leaders accountable, and one that facilitates a healthy level of trust for and dependence on one another, from the executive leaders to the members. We call this "redemptive" polity. It is not the blind trust of the "no brakes" polity, which has a high probability of failure. It is not the lack of trust at the heart of the "parking brake" polity, which promotes corrosive suspicion. Rather, redemptive polity builds on the reality of salvation in Jesus Christ and the indwelling of the Holy Spirit, who is sanctifying both individuals and the church. It wrestles with the reality of stubborn ongoing sinfulness, by building in the proper checks and balances, and by giving leaders the freedom to make mistakes and trust the church's support.

This chapter presents the process and principles that we have developed in our own ministry context. To a large degree, this chapter reflects the evolution of Sojourn Church's polity as it has transitioned into a multichurch. That being said, we believe that many of the things we have learned will be helpful for any church in the process of transitioning into a multichurch and for understanding what is necessary to establish a redemptive polity that enables the church to flourish. We begin with a discussion of two key principles: broadening leadership and understanding the difference between governance and management. Next, we will present the four values that shape a redemptive polity: conviction, trust, collaboration, and empowerment. Then, we will close by providing an illustration of a multichurch polity.

Broadening Leadership

As a church transitions to a multichurch model, it must understand the importance of broadening its leadership. The goal of any polity is to govern the church in a manner worthy of the gospel—for the care of God's people and the accomplishment of his mission. Built correctly, such governance should promote unity and trust among the entire church. Multichurch models exist because of the conviction that churches can do more together than they can do on their own. Such models enable leaders to learn from one another, afford opportunities to gather and equip better leaders, and spread these leaders' influence across a broader community.

During the transition to a multichurch model, it is common for restructuring to occur as the church grows to multiple locations and the overall complexity of the organization increases. The added multiplicity and complexity often drives organizations to reduce the number of decision-makers in order to streamline the decision-making process. This allows organizations to respond to change quickly, but it has the downside of decreasing ownership among the broader leadership of the church. The lack of ownership can have a devastating effect on a church. It can lead to a lack of accountability for those leaders at the top or an unwillingness on the part of the other leaders to take on additional responsibilities. Sadly, this scenario has played out far too often in recent years with several prominent multisite churches. To avoid these tragedies, multichurch models should seek creative ways of broadening the basis of leadership and providing representation on the highest leadership teams from each cooperative or collective church.

Understanding Governance and Management

Governance and management are not the same, although they are often confused with one another. *Governance* is the task of envisioning and planning the framework and parameters of the work to be done. Governing bodies do this by providing vision, procedures, and policies, as well as reviewing vision and program outcomes. *Management* is the task of organizing and overseeing the work, engaging day-to-day in the details of implementation. In a small church, it is common for both functions to be the responsibility of a small leadership team that deals with just a handful of issues. As the church grows in multiplicity, complexity, and budgeting, it is wise to separate governance and management for the sake of clarity and integrity.

In a large church, the failure to separate these two tasks creates "circular" leadership, or what is sometimes called "governance-management." This is when the team that implements the work (management) is the same group that establishes the framework of the work (governance). Circular leadership is problematic because it leads to a leadership environment where it is dangerously easy to adjust the boundaries that establish the framework whenever the church fails to meet expectations or crosses a particular line. In turn, it tends to lead to poor decisions and a lack of adequate controls. It can fuel distrust within the congregation or, in some cases, facilitate the abuse of power by those in leadership.

Another polity we advise church leaders to avoid is *external governance*. In recent years, it has become vogue for large multisite churches to establish governing boards made up of external directors, usually successful leaders of megachurches or other large multisite churches.

The argument supporting this structure claims that it requires a different level of thinking and decision making to lead a large church, and more advanced leaders are necessary to govern these larger churches. While that might be true, these external leaders must rely on secondhand information to lead, which is problematic. It is false to assume that external boards can govern in an unbiased way when the information they use to oversee is filtered through the church's management team.

When leadership difficulties developed at Mars Hill in Seattle, one of the former members of the church's Board of Activity and Accountability, Paul Tripp, recognized this concern. He expressed his chagrin about six months before the situation at Mars Hill imploded and the church was dismantled:

> It became clear to me that a distant, external accountability board can never work well because it isn't a firsthand witness to the ongoing life and ministry of the church. Such a board at best can provide financial accountability, but it will find it very difficult to provide the kind of hands-on spiritual direction and protection that every Christian pastor needs. Unwittingly what happens is that the external accountability board becomes an inadequate replacement for a biblically functioning internal elder board that is the way God designed his church to be led and pastors to be guided and protected.[1]

In light of these concerns, we encourage multichurch models to separate the two functions of governance and management, trusting that God has ordained and equipped the leaders needed to lead and implement the vision of the church.

Values Shaping Polity

Though it is not a guarantee against serious error and even church collapse, a redemptive polity fosters an environment for maturity and multiplication. This redemptive polity is shaped by four values: conviction, trust, collaboration, and empowerment. Let's consider each of these in turn.

Value #1: Conviction

Polity should be biblically grounded, theologically sound, wise, and faithful to God's character and his intention for the church. As noted earlier, Scripture has much to say about those who lead; therefore, governance should be the responsibility of those who meet the qualifications—the call, character, and competencies—as set forth in 1 Timothy 3:1–7 and Titus 1:5–9 (for elders) and 1 Timothy 3:8–13 (for deacons and deaconesses). A sound governing structure should lead to mature decisions and a significant impact for the gospel. Such a polity creates a system with clear oversight and fair representation for all the cooperative or collective churches, while maintaining the ability to be nimble, creative, and effective as one church. In all of this, trust is needed.

Value #2: Trust

Trust may be the most crucial value to cultivate in multichurch governance. As a church increases in multiplicity and complexity, its polity needs to foster trust both structurally (as far as any organization can prompt such trust) and spiritually, pointing leaders to rely on the Spirit for harmony and to work diligently to maintain this Spirit-given unity. In a context of trust, church leaders rely on one another, and members believe rightly, not blindly, that their leaders are called by God, as mature, capable, and wise people acting for the good of the church. Trust is most keenly needed when the inevitable mistakes are made. Within a culture of trust, the church refuses to condemn and, in a knee-jerk overreaction, get rid of "the problem." Moreover, trust is expressed through complementary roles working in collaboration.

Value #3: Collaboration

Governance should promote collaboration throughout the church. As already discussed, collaboration relies on ownership in leaders and members. To focus on the former, every pastor/elder bears responsibility for the church and should have the opportunity to participate in its oversight. In particular this structure invites the lead pastors of the interdependent churches (cooperative model) or the independent collaborating churches (collective model), and perhaps other qualified elders, into the decision-making process. Thus, this polity provides a better, broader representation in major determinations, thereby encouraging its leaders in ownership and collaboration. And collaboration needs empowerment.

Value #4: Empowerment

Leaders require the requisite authority to carry out their responsibilities—decision making, leading, teaching—as spelled out by the church's polity. However, it is not the church's government that grants such empowerment. Rather, God himself gives authority to church leaders to do their responsibilities. Moreover, in the case of congregationally governed churches, members also have certain responsibilities. Accordingly, they possess the God-given authority to carry out those tasks. Empowerment, therefore, is a divine gift. Leaders possess authority and must be able to exercise that power in their spheres of responsibilities. It follows that members cannot usurp their leaders' authority. When members possess authority, they must be able to exercise that power in their sphere of responsibilities. Leaders, then, are not to usurp the members' authority. Most importantly, all power and authority belong to Jesus Christ, who is the head of the church. The church should consciously submit its decision making, leading, teaching, and other responsibilities to the ultimate will of its Lord.

Multichurch Polity at Sojourn Community Church

Rather than present a theoretical model of church governance, we believe it is most helpful to give you a concrete example of multichurch polity. This model represents the polity at Sojourn Community Church, where we serve as leaders. It is only one way of structuring a church's government. It may not be the best way, and it will not fit every church context, but it has the advantage of being an actual polity (and one with which we are very familiar). So we offer it with the hope that it brings clarity and concreteness to this discussion.

Under the headship of Jesus Christ, the leadership council (LC) at Sojourn is responsible for the governance of the church. Specifically, it delivers vision, procedures, and policies, as well as reviews vision and program outcomes. The LC serves the full council of elders (FCE) and the church membership by providing representation for decisions that determine the direction of the church overall. It serves the executive elders (EE) by providing accountability and feedback on vision and the day-to-day management of the church. Thus, this polity includes a management group (EE) within the governing group (LC). Sojourn made the decision not to establish two separate groups (as is often the case in many churches) but to put the responsibility for management in governance. We did this because it seemed logical for the best strategic minds to be present when we discussed future vision and strategy. However, to avoid circular governance (as we talked about earlier), the leadership council is designed to ensure that the executive elders can never hold a majority. The collaborative relationships between the three elder bodies—executive elders, leadership council, and full council of elders—can be diagrammed as follows:

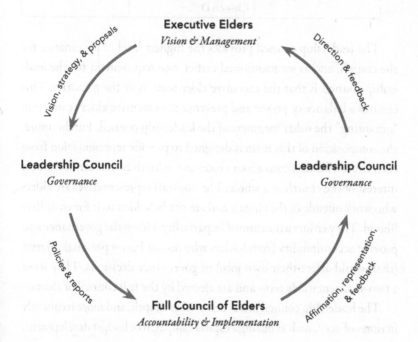

Executive Elders
Vision & Management

Vision, strategy & propsals

Direction & feedback

Leadership Council
Governance

Leadership Council
Governance

Policies & reports

Affirmation, representation & feedback

Full Council of Elders
Accountability & Implementation

As diagrammed above, these three elder bodies collaborate together. But the diagram does not give you a clear picture of what these three leadership teams do. And you may be wondering: is there a role for a lead pastor, and where does that fit?

Leadership Council (LC)

The leadership council is made up of leaders comprised of the following groups: the executive elders, the lead pastors of the four interdependent churches, and a minimum of two nonstaff elders elected from the FCE.[2]

Executive Elders	Lead Pastors of the Four Churches	Non-Staff Representatives
Preaching and Vision	Church A	Minimum of Two
Churches and Ministries	Church B	
Operations and Finances	Church C	
	Church D	

The leadership council provides the highest level of governance for the church, and as we mentioned earlier, one requirement for the leadership council is that the executive elder team is in the minority. This ensures a balance of power and prevents the executive elder team from "outvoting" the other members of the leadership council. Furthermore, the composition of this team is designed to provide representation from each church for decisions about vision and initiatives that are in the best interest of the church as a whole. The nonstaff representatives are elders who work outside of the church and are not beholden to it for their livelihood. They ensure a measure of impartiality within the governance and provide accountability from leaders who do not have a personal interest (that would affect their own jobs) in governance decisions. They serve a two-year renewable term and are elected by the full council of elders.

The leadership council meets every other month, and more frequently in times of need, such as during a capital campaign or budget development.

The executive elders and the lead pastors each appoint a representative to establish the agenda for these meetings and to prepare the minutes which are, along with the monthly mission metrics report, distributed to the full council of elders.[3] The leadership council's responsibilities are as follows:

1. The exercise of governance
2. The establishment of governing policies
3. The ratification of annual vision and goals for ministries and churches
4. The review of the progress of ministries
5. The deliberation and development of key initiatives

The LC makes the ultimate decisions regarding the annual budget, the preaching calendar, capital and ministry campaigns, and plans for expansion. Furthermore, the LC produces and delivers bimonthly meeting minutes, the yearly budget proposal as voted on by the FCE, a set of annual goals and performance plans, and clear expansion proposals when they are applicable.

Full Council of Elders (FCE)

The full council of elders (FCE) consists of all the elders: the executive elders, the lead pastors of the four churches, and all the other elders of those four churches. It overlaps with the leadership council by including the executive elders and the lead pastors of the churches, but it represents the full elder body—all the elders from all the churches. The full council of elders is responsible for care and governance. This involves shepherding, as the elders disciple the members toward maturity in Christ, care for them and their needs, equip them for ministry, help them stay connected in community, and keep them on mission. Every elder is part of a particular church elder team and is accountable to their lead pastor at that church. The multichurch structure fosters specialization by encouraging elders to serve in their areas of giftedness.

In terms of governance, the elders are responsible collectively for the oversight of all aspects of church life and ministry. They appoint deacons, deaconesses, and other ministry leaders at their particular church. At the same time, their specific leadership responsibilities are based on their gifting and capacity, so some governing functions are delegated to the teams of elders mentioned earlier: the executive elders and the leadership council. The FCE also votes to approve or oppose the proposals submitted to them, and its members participate in standing and ad hoc committees. Finally, the FCE is a forum for elders and leaders to share input and concerns, including a grievance process to make formal objections.

We want to call attention to this last element, because we have found that a grievance process is integral to healthy polity within the multichurch model. It provides a process by which any elder can address concerns with the behavior and/or decision of the leadership council or the executive elders (see appendix 1 for more details).

Executive Elders (EE)

The executive elders serve as the senior leadership team and have the primary responsibility for the day-to-day operation of the entire church. Subject to the approval of the leadership council, the executive elders have authority over the budget, hiring and firing of staff, facility development, and use and other operational needs of the church. They are appointed by the lead pastor (who also serves as an executive elder) and affirmed by the full council of elders. The focus of the executive elders is on the church as a whole, promoting unity between the congregations, drawing people to the church, and leading the mission forward. They lead, develop, and provide catalytic oversight. Specifically, the responsibilities of the EE are providing day-to-day oversight of the church through strategic leadership, supervision of church staff, and development of plans for expansion. The executive elders are expected to produce strategic proposals for the leadership council to review, develop monthly mission metrics, and handle staff reviews.

Lead Pastor

Some multichurches will be directed by a lead pastor who is appointed by the full council of elders. He functions as the first among equals.[4]

The lead pastor leads the full council of elders and the church through casting vision, overseeing the ministry of preaching, fostering sound theology, and praying. He also has oversight of the executive elder team. His deliverables include a yearly "calling" plan—his sense of God's direction for the church—complete with quarterly goals, as well as a two-year running preaching schedule, which is permanent three months out from the present.

The leadership council. The full council of elders. The executive elders. These three elder bodies collaborate together and are responsible for the governance of the church as a whole. But they are not the only structures for governance—they comprise the central authority. Governance structures also exist for the individual cooperative and collective churches within the multichurch, and these structures include the local lead pastors, the local elder teams, and the local leadership teams.

Local Lead Pastors (LLP)

The local lead pastors are the leading (and usually preaching) elders at the individual churches of the multichurch. They develop and execute a contextualized vision and mission for their church that is derivative of the broad vision of the whole church. Their plan is developed with the help of their local elder team (LET) and in collaboration with the other local lead pastors. Additionally, they lead their LET and provide pastoral oversight for their members. They must possess a unique mixture of gifts and abilities that allow them to fulfill the duties of a lead pastor of a church, while humbly submitting to the overall leadership of the church as a whole.

The local lead pastors are responsible for the leadership of their local church and are the primary communicators for that church. They develop its vision and handle the formation and leadership of the local leadership team (discussed below). They also manage the local staff and the budget for that church. Their deliverables include a locally contextualized ministry plan that is aligned with the overall ministry plan, a budget for staffing and ministry, and the completion of mission metrics for their local church. They are also responsible for annual assessments of the local staff.

Local Elder Teams (LET)

The polity of the individual churches within the multichurch also has local elder teams who are responsible for the governance of those churches. They exercise their leadership through either active participation or delegation to other leadership teams. The local elder teams confirm the formation and composition of the local leadership team (to be discussed next) and handle approval of the annual church budget. They also develop and execute a local ministry plan. The members of each LET also belong to the full council of elders, whose duties were mentioned earlier.

Local Leadership Teams (LLT)

The local leadership teams are responsible for providing direction and management for their local church. Their composition is determined by the particularities of their church. The local lead pastor, working in conjunction with his local elder team, bears the primary responsibility for the formation and leadership of the LLT. Because the leadership council provides accountability and covering for the local churches, specific non-staff participation in the LLT is not required, but it is not discouraged either. This also means that the dual responsibilities of governance and management do not need to be separated at the local church level, unless such separation is desired.

The local leadership teams handle the establishment of the church's contextualized vision and mission, as a derivative of the larger vision and mission of the church as a whole. They also execute that vision and mission through the mobilization of staff, lay elders, volunteers, and members. They develop key initiatives for the health and growth of the local church. They formulate local policies in conjunction with the local elder team to address situations and circumstances where the policies of the leadership council have not spoken directly. This, again, emphasizes the need for contextualized ministry rather than a one-size-fits-all approach guided by a central authority. The local leadership teams develop an annual budget alongside a ministry plan that they submit to the leadership council and the financial accountability team. They also provide an annual review of the staff and keep minutes of meetings in which any significant decisions are made (for example, capital investments and staff changes).

Local lead pastors. Local elder teams. Local leadership teams. These three leadership structures collaborate together and are responsible for the governance of the individual churches within the multichurch. There is one further layer of leadership, however, that serves these leadership teams. Several other groups operate under the oversight of the local pastors, elders, and leadership teams.

Deacons, Deaconesses, and Other Leadership Responsibilities

Deacons and deaconesses are responsible for leading the many (nonelder level) ministries of the churches. These may include community groups, hospitality, missions, children, youth, mercy, women's and men's Bible studies, equipping classes (e.g., theology, pastoral care, membership, financial planning), and worship. Local elder teams nominate qualified members who are proven servants to become deacons and deaconesses. These men and women must meet the qualifications as set forth in 1 Timothy 3:8–13.

When needed, the leadership council may also constitute additional teams of elders and nonelders. These auxiliary teams serve in a particular capacity until their work is completed. Two examples of this are the financial advisory team, which provides expertise for the budgeting process, and the executive elder compensation review team, which evaluates the executive elders and advises the financial advisory team on their annual compensation. These two teams protect the executive elders from a conflict of interest regarding the budget.

Finally, while our attention to this point has focused on governance matters and leadership structures, we cannot neglect the importance of a healthy church body. If a multichurch is an elder-led, deacon- and deaconess-served, and congregation-affirming church, then its members must have clearly delineated responsibilities as well. At Sojourn, members are responsible to affirm the annual budget and any significant increases to it (as a whole church), and to approve any amendments to the articles of incorporation and bylaws (that apply to the whole church).

The members of a particular local church confirm their own elders and affirm any budget proposal to purchase land or real estate for their church. In addition to these governance duties, members bear the responsibility to participate in the implementation of the vision and ministry of the church.

The Macropolity and Micropolity Dynamics

Multichurch models feature church polity at both a macrolevel (in our example, the LC, FCE, and EE) and a microlevel (the LLP, LET, and LLT). It is important to clarify exactly how these two levels of polity relate to one another in the overall government of the church. There are several key connections linking the macrolevel to the microlevel. First, the leadership council provides accountability and covering for the particular churches. It offers collaborative space for these churches to develop their contextualized vision and mission, ensuring that those are in harmony (not uniformity) with one another and with the vision and mission of the church overall. The leadership council also supplies a feedback loop for the executive elders regarding the growth and expansion of the churches.

Second, the executive elders relate primarily to the churches through the local lead pastors. They consult and coach these pastors in the development of their churches and promote collaboration among those churches. The local lead pastors, in turn, are part of the leadership council and play a crucial role in the governance of the church overall. They contribute directly to the establishment of vision, direction, procedures, and policies, and to the review of vision and program outcomes. Their service on the leadership council provides representation from each church for vision, decisions, and initiatives, and it is carried out in the best interests of the church as a whole. And like all other elders, the local lead pastors serve on the full council of elders.

Since all the local elder teams serve on the full council of elders, they are in a place where they can affirm or amend the vision, direction, procedures, and policies that the leadership council proposes. The full council of elders is the opportunity for all the elders, representing their particular churches, to govern the church as a whole.

Multichurch Polity

Because of the multiplicity and complexity of multichurch models, they require a polity that is far more intricate than the government of most churches. After reading through the various groups and teams at both the macro- and microlevels, you might think that the degree of complexity in this church polity is unnecessarily burdensome or inefficient. However, whereas ease and efficiency are American cultural values, we are not convinced they are biblical virtues. In the formation of this intricate polity, we guard against two extremes—the "no brakes" polity and the "parking brake" polity—and instead promote a redemptive polity. This approach takes into consideration two parallel realities:

1. The church has been redeemed by Jesus Christ.
2. The church is being redeemed by Jesus Christ.

The first point tells us that our polity should be structured to reflect and promote a high level of trust in, and expectation for, its leaders. The second point reminds us that our polity must acknowledge the fallen condition of our leaders and thus provide the appropriate checks and balances. As we developed this polity, we realized that the multiplicity and complexity of multichurch models promotes a broadening of the leadership structure so as to prepare the church for maturity and multiplication. A growing and expanding multichurch fosters ownership, encourages all members to participate according to their giftedness, and focuses on expansion, thereby requiring a deepening pool of leaders. Redemptive polity makes provision for the broadening of leadership.

A word of advice: don't get lost in the details! Rather, understand the purpose and function of these various structures, then contextualize them for your multichurch model. Our multichurch polity came into existence for reasons specific to our context. We were responding to the issues we faced, as outlined in chapter 1. While we are only a few years in, we have found these changes to be profoundly helpful for our organization. Finally, do not forget a key axiom for church government: great character overcomes the weakest polity, and poor character undermines the strongest polity.

MultiMinistry

We have looked at issues of structure and polity, and it is now time to focus on the ministries within the multichurch model. Ephesians 4 details how God gives gifted leaders to prepare the church for the works of ministry. But what is ministry? Ministry is simply *what the church does*: worship, discipleship, prayer, mission, care, education, mercy, and much more. Multichurches present certain challenges to ministry because of the ongoing dynamic between the one church and the multiple cooperating or collective churches. This dynamic makes building synergy between and within ministries significantly more difficult for multichurches than for most pillar or multisite churches. For example, in a pillar model church, the vision, strategy, and expression of ministry may be determined and executed by one person—the pastor—or a small group of people. Multichurch models change this completely.

Before we look at ministry in a multichurch model, however, we first want to discuss ministry in the different multisite models so we can contrast between the two approaches. Then we will explore how multichurch models can better face the challenges specific to multisite models by developing philosophy spectrums and graduated expectations. Next, we will discuss three categories of ministry priorities in multichurch models: foundational, core, and particular ministries. Finally, we will look at the development of particular ministries by focusing on the issue of empowerment and experimentation, and the need to foster a culture where failure is normal and encouraged as part of faithful risk.

Challenges in Multisite Ministry

How do you oversee ministry in a multisite church? Many multisite churches use a central team of experts. When Sojourn Community Church was operating with a federation multisite model, we called this group our global ministry team. The idea behind this group was simple. Leaders in particular ministry fields served the whole church. Thus, each local congregation benefited from the expertise of these ministry leaders in a way far outreaching what they could afford on their own as a small church. It was like having a team of consultants on retainer—all for a fraction of the cost. It was ingenious . . . if not for the demands of reality.

A year into this model our church leaders began to grow frustrated with the response of the campuses, especially the smaller ones. The global ministry leaders felt that the campuses did not appreciate the benefits of the oversight and did not realize how good they had it. After all, the campuses had free access to some great minds with deep experience on a wide variety of topics, such as counseling, mercy, community, kids, women, and international missions ministries. And they had access whenever they wanted! Yet the campus leaders kept complaining about the perceived lack of value they were getting for their dollar.

Greater understanding came as we talked about what it would mean to become a multichurch and how that shift would affect our financial and ministry models. The central church leadership began to realize that although the quality of the global ministry team was amazing, and these consultants were more than eager to serve the local churches, they were rarely used by the smaller congregations. And the reason was ridiculously obvious. Our smaller congregations did not have the staff to take full advantage of these ministry leaders. Why? Because they were not yet at the place to develop their ministries at that high of a level. Certainly these ministries would matter someday, but not right now.

This exposed a major weakness in our vision of global ministry consultants. Our goal had been to combine resources from all our churches to accomplish something we could not do individually. Our larger churches subsidized the smaller ones by carrying a disproportionate amount of the cost to have such a team. The smaller churches were not staffed to take advantage of this team, so the opposite was actually happening. Our smaller campuses were contributing financially to support a global ministry team primarily used by our larger campuses. Although we had intended the opposite, for all intents and purposes the reality was that the smaller campuses were subsidizing the ministry of our larger campuses. Everything was functioning in reverse. This revelation led us to rethink how we collaborated between ministries so as not to overtax our smaller congregations by providing superfluous services to them.

An additional problem faced by multisite churches is the ministry "bottleneck." The ministry bottleneck refers to the requirement that campus leaders need approval from the global team before doing anything. In our case the leaders at our campuses felt that every decision needed to be approved, and even in cases where no permission was needed, the mere existence of the structure created a culture of uncertainty. This led to hesitation and eventually the stagnation of ministry at the local level.

Moving away from this culture was not without its own risks. Having control meant we could create consistency and ensure quality, two leadership values that are beneficial to ministry. The cost of that control was steep, however, not only in terms of energy and dollars but also in the reduction of ministry. Campus leaders avoided new ideas and ministry opportunities because of the annoyance of red tape. And when they attempted creative ideas and failed, the disappointment of failure often shut things down.

Multichurch Ministry

These challenges were realities as we struggled with a multisite model for ministry. As we explored the idea of multichurch, we also explored a different approach to ministry. As our maxim states, multichurch exists for its churches. Therefore, these models push ministry to take place in their cooperative or collective churches. Rather than having a centralized leadership group that dictates vision, strategy, and expression of ministry to the churches, multichurch fosters collaboration between them. The leadership council determines the overall vision with representation from each church. Ministry leaders at each church build the strategy. Each church executes the expression of that strategy and has freedom to decide which ministries to feature (remember, everything cannot matter) and how to contextualize those ministries for its particular location. Because of the heightened emphasis on collaboration in vision and strategy, the multichurch can count on significant local ownership as well as a substantial degree of similarity in expression without exerting heavy centralized control. The goal of multichurch is to develop and execute a global vision, a unified strategy, and a contextualized expression of ministry. As our third maxim emphasizes, multiplication is always nonnegotiable.

Teams of staff and volunteers from each church develop and execute a unified strategy, working together to align the strategy of a particular ministry (e.g., community groups, kids, and missions) with the overall vision of the church. These teams seek to build a consensus on strategy, share the best practices, and use local experiences to refine the strategy and vision for their particular ministry.

But two steep challenges face these teams. First, their leaders may have differences in conviction and experience, and these differences can create tension in an environment emphasizing ownership. Second, a multichurch rarely consists of churches of similar sizes and resources. These dissimilarities affect the execution of ministries in the churches. Multichurches can overcome these challenges by developing philosophy spectrums and graduated expectations.

Philosophy Spectrums

A basic truth of empowerment is that when people are given options, they tend to use them. This makes the management of multiple ministries in multiple churches particularly challenging for multichurches. One goal of a multichurch is the empowerment of each church and its leaders to develop contextualized ministries that reflect the gifting of the church and the needs of the community. This is opposed to offering a little bit of everything and, conversely, focusing exclusively on the priorities set by the church overall (one size fits all). This empowerment affords a strong measure of freedom;

therefore, it can lead to a fair amount of divergence from a unified ministry. Controlling this diversity is costly and can also be frustrating. Moreover, it is unnecessary. In actuality, appropriate diversity in ministry philosophy strengthens rather than weakens the church. That said, we understand that church splits often begin over issues that start as differences in philosophy. Multichurches need to live with this tension, instead of trying to resolve it.[1]

One tool helping Sojourn to live with this tension is a philosophy spectrum. One philosophy spectrum is developed for each ministry. A philosophy spectrum identifies the range of comfortable divergence within church practice. For each spectrum, there is an inner core, which indicates the expressions of ministry upon which the church completely agrees. Around that inner core, the church draws outside borders to indicate what kinds of ministries are permitted. The core and the borders are determined by the overall church's leadership council, with representatives from each cooperative or collective church. Each local church is free to develop contextualized expressions of ministry within the approved philosophy spectrum.

The following is an example of a philosophy spectrum regarding how to provide care and counseling in a church:

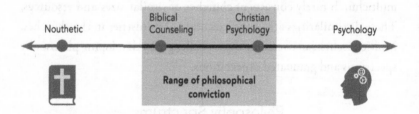

This philosophy spectrum approximates the range of divergence for engaging in the ministry of care and counseling at Sojourn. On the left side of the spectrum is what is commonly called nouthetic counseling, often associated with older, more traditional forms of biblical counseling that reject anything that is not explicitly taught in Scripture. On the right side we find secular psychology, which operates from a nonbiblical foundation. Biblical counseling and Christian psychology are two intermediate camps.

A church may embrace a spectrum of these philosophies. In a pillar model church, the care and counseling spectrum will often be quite narrow, limited to one specific approach. But in multichurch models, such a restricted philosophy creates unnecessary control and limits the strength that comes from different perspectives. A multichurch leadership council determines the range of philosophical convictions that are allowed for matters of care and counseling, and in this example, the spectrum extends from biblical counseling to Christian psychology. The church is comfortable with and promotes ministries within this range, but it excludes ministries that fall outside this range, including both nouthetic and secular counseling approaches.

A philosophy spectrum communicates how much something matters while also providing room for different perspectives on the local leadership teams. The spectrums for some ministries may be rather narrowly delineated, while the spectrums of other ministries may be fairly broad. In this way, a multichurch can provide boundaries for each ministry while allowing for a range of differences. Because narrow ranges can exert more control than needed and broad ranges can lead to significant divergence, the leadership council should carefully set clear ranges with which the church is comfortable.

Graduated Expectations

When I (Brad) played tennis in high school, Andre Agassi was at the pinnacle of his tennis career. I always resonated with Agassi's aggressive and slightly rebellious style. In 2010, he published *Open: An Autobiography*. I was fascinated by the stories of his epic matches and the struggles that came with being a professional tennis player. They gave me insight into what it takes to be one of the best in the world.

Agassi's story is also heartbreaking, as he recounts what it was like to grow up as a child prodigy in tennis. He was never given the chance to just be a kid and engage in normal childhood activities. The storyline is a familiar one for many child prodigies, and it is shared by children from broken homes, those who live through tragic circumstances, and those who have overly demanding parents. Hearing these stories, we universally feel a sense of loss for those children. We know that growing up too early robs children of joy during a life stage in which they should be free of worries and responsibilities. Usually, at the right time and in the right environment, people learn to take on responsibilities—schooling, career, marriage, family, home ownership—and this development is exciting and a joy in itself. As people grow into their abilities and gifts, expectations increase and appropriate responsibilities follow.

We find that this pattern of maturation is true for growing churches as well. A challenge for multichurch models is that the expectations for local congregations are often set beyond the ability of those churches. This dilemma occurs because the church as a whole has typically existed for some time—usually over a decade—and thus has a well-developed vision along with the convictions and skills to execute it. When the church launches new cooperating churches or adds new collective churches, they are rarely equipped to keep up with the whole church in terms of finances and resources. If the church as a whole fails to recognize this reality, then it develops unreasonable expectations and demands. The effect is like robbing a child of her childhood. The new church loses some of the joy of growing up, learning new things, and growing into new responsibilities. All of this is overshadowed by the weight of unrealistic expectations.

So how do you avoid this? By developing *graduated expectations*. These are progressively increasing hopes and prospects for new cooperating or collective churches. Graduated expectations allow these new churches to grow up properly. A three-year-old church is permitted to be a three-year-old church.[2] To demand that a three-year-old church must have all the ministries of the ten-year-old originating church is to sentence it to feelings of perpetual failure. Just as a young person learns to grow into maturity and take on new responsibilities, a young church needs to grow into its own as well. Every person and every organization needs time and space to learn and grow.

Time and size are the two factors that determine a church's ability to successfully develop a particular ministry. *Time* is a factor because developing a particular ministry takes an extensive season to envision the ministry, establish its strategic plan, wrestle with its philosophy spectrum, and identify and train its staff and volunteers. Attempting to start multiple ministries too early puts undue stress on all these elements, especially on the people engaged in those ministries. In this regard, the maxim "everything cannot matter" is key. It is wiser to do a few ministries well rather than to attempt unsuccessfully to do everything.

Size is a factor because developing a particular ministry requires the church to allocate resources to that ministry. These resources include finances, prayer, enthusiasm and energy, staff and volunteers, and the like. Generally speaking, the larger the size of the church, the more resources it has to dedicate to ministry. As a church grows, it can dedicate more resources and develop more ministries.

Connecting time and size, the following chart illustrates graduated expectations (this chart is representative and not exhaustive):

Years	1–2	3–4	5–6	6+
Attendance	0–100	100–200	200–500	500–1,000+
Foundational Ministries	Sunday Service	Sunday Service	Sunday Service	Sunday Service
	Community Groups	Community Groups	Community Groups	Community Groups
	Kids' Ministry	Kids' Ministry	Kids' Ministry	Kids' Ministry
Core Ministries		Care Ministry	Care Ministry	Care Ministry
		Youth Ministry	Youth Ministry	Youth Ministry
			International Missions	International Missions
			Mercy Ministry	Mercy Ministry
				Men's and Women's programs
				College Ministry
Particular ministries		Choir	Tutoring	Outdoors Ministry
			Sports	Sports programs
				Choir

Time and size are correlated with three categories of ministry priorities in multichurch models: foundational, core, and particular ministries.

Foundational ministries constitute the bare minimum of what it means to be a cooperative or collective church. Thinking back to the conviction-urgency chart and the conviction-ability chart in chapter 6, these are Quadrant I ministries. They express the essence of the church's DNA, and every new church must have these in place before it is launched.

Core ministries constitute the growth engine of a cooperative or collective church. These are the ministries in Quadrant II and are expected of all the churches, as soon as they gain the necessary ability to engage in them. In this way, the church as a whole flourishes with an irreducible complexity. Core ministries express the broader elements of the church's DNA.

Particular ministries constitute the unique expressions of a cooperative or collective church. These are ministries in Quadrant III—unrequired yet distinct of a particular church as it contextualizes for its location. These ministries are born out of a church's conviction as developed by its local leadership team.

Multichurch models resist ecclesiological reductionism. Specifically, the whole church avoids such reductionism, but not because all its churches feature every ministry. Rather, all its churches have the foundational ministries, all of them are moving toward having all the core ministries, and some of its churches engage in particular ministries according to their contextualization needs. This approach means that the newer and smaller churches are not expected to engage in every core ministry from the outset. A multichurch might have a mercy ministry in one of its congregations, for example, and this initiative provides opportunities for members of the newer and smaller churches to give financially, use their gifts, and join in that ministry until their own local church can develop a mercy ministry for itself.

Accordingly, graduated expectations reduce the stress on newer and smaller churches to live up to the expectations of both the church as a whole and its larger churches. The structure allows the smaller churches to develop new ministries when they are ready and as they have the requisite resources. Additionally, dividing these ministries into three categories of priority helps to determine what matters, how much it matters, and when it matters for ministries within multichurch models.

Development of Particular Ministries

The development of particular ministries in multichurch models requires further explanation. Because this feature is rarely found in multisite models, a deeper discussion of it may help to distinguish a multisite and multichurch model.

Empowerment and Experimentation

Particular ministries—unique expressions of a cooperative or collective church—arise from a multichurch's commitment to multiplication and the empowerment of its churches. This dual obligation stimulates a culture of freedom and innovation that rarely exists in control-centered multisite models. According to the biblical vision set forth in Ephesians 4, all the members of the body of Christ should be using their God-given gifts to proclaim the gospel and to further the maturity and multiplication of the church. Regretfully, many churches limit the use of these gifts out of fear. And even when churches have good intentions and want to encourage the gifts of members, they sometimes mistake opportunities for their members to serve as inconveniences. This mistake leads churches to design ministries that take the burden off of their members and place it onto their leaders. But this prevents church members from fully using their gifts.

This phenomenon is seen when a multichurch, rather than identifying, training, and mobilizing its members for care and mercy ministries, hires a professional counselor and a neighborhood-development expert to carry out those ministries. Such a decision is motivated by the desire to avoid burdening the churches' members with responsibility or to avoid having the staff inconvenienced by less experienced members trying to do ministry. Therefore, professionals are contracted to reduce the burden. This thinking discourages members from using their gifts in a fulfilling and God-honoring way.

Because the church is a body (Eph. 4:1–16; 1 Cor. 12:12–26), it is healthiest when every part is functioning properly and together. Leaders ministering alongside members, all of whom are participating, is the healthy way to do ministry. This is the multichurch vision for particular ministries. It starts by creating and fostering a culture that celebrates innovation. As the church resources the cooperating or collective churches and as it is judicious on what really matters, it encourages great diversity in the expression of ministry. Opportunities for the expression of spiritual gifts expand as the church extends into different contexts, which enables members of the larger church body to find a specific place to use their gifts. These particular ministries provide flavor and nuance to the expression of gifts, and they encourage innovation and ownership.

Nathan, a church member and former DJ, had a passion for serving the marginalized in the city. He wanted to build a ministry connecting church members to the hurting members of the community around them. It would have been easy for the church to determine that such a ministry would be too costly or outside the scope of its mission. Fortunately, it did not. With a desire to push passionate members to use their gifts, the church gave resources to Nathan and his team, so they could lead the way in mercy. He built a growing ministry that serves the multichurch as a whole, while being predominantly housed within one local church. Members from the multichurch's local congregations are able to participate in works of mercy. His ministry eventually outgrew the church and now supports other churches around the country. Empowering Nathan and members like him to experiment and use their gifts blesses the whole church (and many others).

If the idea of releasing control of a particular ministry makes you uncomfortable, multichurch models offer some peace of mind. Because the experimentation is happening at the local level, divergences in ministry philosophy have a fairly limited effect on the church as a whole. At the same time, innovations that show promising results can always be elevated and shared with the rest of the churches. Encouraging particular ministries fosters innovation, creativity, and freedom. And it allows for contextualization at the local level, which minimizes the risk of changing the larger church vision and allows the church to adopt new approaches whenever they need.

It's Okay to Fail

When you develop an empowered culture where people feel free to experiment with new ways to advance the gospel and multiply the church, you will inevitably encounter failure. Part of promoting this culture is allowing people to fail—and to celebrate them when they do. Entrepreneurs in the business world know the importance of having a culture that permits and celebrates failure. Edward Hess, Professor of Business Administration at the Darden Graduate School of Business, makes this point:

> Innovation is the result of iterative learning processes as well as environments that encourage experimentation, critical inquiry, critical debate, and accept failures as a necessary part of the process. Yes, I said failures. Failure is a necessary part of the innovation process because from failure comes learning, iteration, adaptation, and the building of new conceptual and physical models through an iterative learning process. Almost all innovations are the result of prior learning from failures.[3]

This is also true for the church. While the gospel itself needs and permits no innovation, the means by which it is communicated *always* demands contextualization. Just as the gospel is contextualized, so too is the church that emerges from it. As diverse members use their gifts to accomplish the mission and minister in and through their churches, they will both underadapt and overadapt to the culture. At times, these ministries bear fruit; at other times, they crash and burn. Building a multichurch characterized by empowerment and freedom requires a culture that permits failure and celebrates the creative impulse behind it.

Many large and successful churches have a difficult time with this. It may be related to the church's leadership and the need leaders feel to avoid failures. To put it simply, leaders don't like to fail. It is difficult for leaders to permit failure because of how it reflects on them. This fear can cause them to have an unhealthy view of failure, and instead of seeing failure as the natural result of creative experimentation, they despise it. But as followers of Jesus and leaders in his church, we need to remember that our identity is secure in Christ. It is Jesus who is building his church, and his desire is to see every member find their place and minister within it. Therefore, we can take ourselves less seriously and stop trying to manufacture our own success and minimize opportunities for failure. Moreover, this frees us to empower members to exercise their gifts and participate in particular ministries. As Hess notes,

> Innovative organizations build the right culture and enabling internal system that drives innovation behaviors. Along with mindsets and system come the right experimental processes. But underlying all of this is one key concept: you must be willing to accept failures as a necessary part of the innovation process. Why do many large companies buy their innovation? Because their dominant culture of 99% defect-free operational excellence squashes any attempts at innovation just like a Sumo wrestler sitting on a small gymnast. They cannot accept failures. The reality is that failures are a necessary part of innovation.[4]

A multichurch is an innovative movement for the advancement of the gospel and the multiplication of the church. A large part of this innovation involves being willing to let people fail in their pursuits—and celebrating them when they do. This is key to developing a culture of empowerment.

I (Brad) have seen this play out through several years of building community group ministries. Giving group leaders the ability to run their own events, make decisions, and potentially fail, catalyzes creative energy. I have seen concerts fizzle, parties bomb, and service ideas tank. But we have always celebrated the effort and ingenuity, regardless of success. This has led to the willingness of these leaders to try again, resulting in far more successes than failures. Still, those failures made successes possible.

Ministry in a Healthy Multichurch

A healthy multichurch holds a global vision, a unified strategy, and a contextualized expression of the foundational, core, and particular ministries in tension. The tension is what makes multichurch exciting and challenging—at the same time!

Providing clarity and committing to empowerment will lead to unexpected joys. A couple of women in Huntsville start a morning day care to use the blessing of their new building, and now have a waiting list of kids 200 strong. A young woman escapes the sex industry and builds a ministry for other exploited women searching for the same freedom. A businessman uses his resources and connections to provide small business loans to marginalized residents in the inner city. The churches to which these saints belong are blessed because they were empowered to use their gifts. By giving them the freedom to experiment and by accepting failure, a multichurch will find the joy of empowering members in creative ways to advance the gospel.

MultiMoney

"The church is always talking about money! More money for pastors. More money for programs. More money for buildings. It's always about more money!" While this is an overstatement, the criticism is still commonplace. Larger churches are always dealing with the perception that they spend an inordinate amount of time discussing financial matters and appealing for money. If you have been a church leader for any length of time, you know this is part and parcel of the ecclesial landscape.

We certainly do not want to feed this financial frenzy, but we need to address the reality of money and how finances are handled in multichurch models. To begin, we will expose and explode four myths about multisite and finances.

1. The myth of efficiency and lowered costs
2. The myth of control and financial savings
3. The myth of arrival
4. The myth of edge growth

After looking at these four myths, we will introduce an important principle that drives how money is handled in the multichurch model, and look at two aspects of that principle: ownership and moral choices.

The Four Myths of Multisite and Money

"You can become whatever you set your mind on."
"God helps those who help themselves."

Every day we hear platitudes that make promises. People share common sense wisdom that seems true, but when we push and pull on the idea, it doesn't hold up. Myths are powerful, controlling ideas that trick us into believing them. They are fascinating... and frustrating. They can also be stubborn. They grip our hearts and refuse to let go. One reason for such stubbornness is the powerful influence they exert on our lifestyle, our values, our goals, and our dreams. But as powerful as they seem, in the end *myths are not true*. They seem to be true, and we act as if they are true, and many others believe and act on their seeming truthfulness. But they are not, which leads us to make erroneous decisions and avoidable mistakes.

There are several myths that exist in the world of multisite, and in this chapter, we expose four of those myths that relate to finances. We hope seeing these as the fables they are will free us to avoid common mistakes as we approach multichurch finances.

Myth #1: The Myth of Efficiency

Often a church considers multisite or multichurch because it imagines that the *efficiency found in these models will save it money*. This is perhaps the greatest myth of multisite/multichurch, and it has lured many leadership teams into great expectations for their new model. It is easy to believe because it seems logical. If several services/venues/churches are doing similar thing in different locations, surely they can reduce role duplication and save resources by consolidating programs.

But what makes sense as an idea is rarely, if ever, reflected in reality. The reason for this disconnect is a combination of factors related to complexity and control. Multisite and multichurch are complex models, and organizational complexity costs money.[1] The more complex a task, the more training and skill a worker needs to accomplish it and the higher the financial cost. This financial burden is why many businesses spend a good deal of time and money attempting to simplify their organization. This is the driving force behind the innovations in factories and fast food production lines. This is especially true for organizations duplicating their services in many locations.

While companies can reduce their products and simplify their tasks when they are manufacturing widgets, this does not translate to the church. As we saw in chapter 5, there is an irreducible complexity to the church. While the church can simplify programs and even get rid of some, it does not have the luxury of eliminating all complexity without falling into ecclesiological reductionism. Worship, discipleship, mission, care, mercy, prayer, community—a church cannot opt to exclude these ministries without devolving into an irregular church.

This is not to say that multisite and multichurch models do not provide some financial savings. Indeed, there are many areas where the myth of efficiency *almost* appears to be true. Unfortunately, savings in these areas are usually offset by increased costs in other areas. One example is facility costs. In a pillar model church, there is one facility (even if it includes several buildings) and one mortgage/lease. In multisite and multichurch models, there are multiple facilities and multiple mortgages/ leases. Multiple facilities cost more than a single facility. Multiple mortgages/leases bring additional costs. Even in situations where it is cheaper to have four small facilities than one large one, there is an increase in other costs, such as maintenance, insurance, and the administration of multiple vendors and locations. The same principle applies for staffing, communication, and the coordination of ministries across multiple locations or churches. For example, the efficiency of multisite and multichurch models reduces the staffing need at a particular venue or church, but the complexity of managing staff at different locations or in multiple churches increases the need for administrative personnel, human resources, and bookkeeping. Greater complexity costs more money.

Do not fall for the myth of multisite efficiency.

Myth #2: The Myth of Control

A second myth that needs to be exposed is that *greater control results in financial savings*. Earlier, we discussed the matter of complexity. But complexity does not impact multisite and multichurch models equally. The reason is that complexity has a partner in crime: control. With complexity comes the question of how much needs to be controlled, and while complexity is a given, control is a variable. The example of the printed church bulletin in chapter 5 illustrates this point. While the challenge of communications within a multichurch is complex, the level of control we exert determines the scope of the cost. If we want to control the brand of the church by continuing to create unique bulletins each week, we need more communication staff for printing, layout, and distribution. If we relinquish control to local staffs, then we can limit the cost. This illustrates the effect of control on the cost of complexity: the more control there is, the greater the cost of complexity.

As mapped out on our spectrum of multisite and multichurch models, a key difference among the five types of churches is the degree of control exercised by the central leadership. Moving from left to right on the spectrum means empowering more decision making at the level of the particular locations/churches. It also means a reduction of central control. This transition opens the opportunity for greater contextualization and diversity in the particular locations/churches. The lessening of central control also reduces the central cost. Indeed, our research reveals a clear correlation between a model's level of central control and the cost to support its central staff and functions.

The following diagram portrays the (approximate) percentage of the budget of a particular location or particular church that goes to supporting the multisite or multichurch central staff and functions.

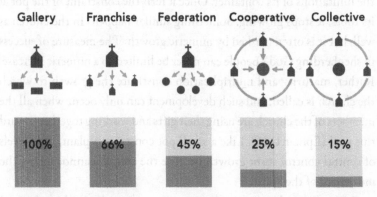

Percentage of local congregation giving needed to support central staff and functions

The higher the demand for a controlled brand and a standardized church experience, the more dollars that must be spent to support that requirement.[2] For example, in a highly controlled franchise model church, the central cost comes from many areas. Video venues, for example, require expensive media equipment to capture and broadcast the weekly message. Complex communication requires additional staff in order to produce all the components required by the multiple locations. The coordination of ministries across multiple locations requires more management staff and administrators. More control requires more money. Again, it is a myth that greater control equals financial savings.

But the myth of control is also problematic if we believe control is a viable way to maintain regulation of a complex organization like the church over the long term. Control has its own cost, which eventually takes a toll on the church. Central control leads to a reduction of vision as it propels the church into the maintenance phase of its lifecycle (see chapter 6). This outcome can happen even as the church continues to multiply venues or churches and to increase in overall attendance and giving. The church may be growing externally, but the financial strain is causing premature aging.

In addition, control is ultimately unattainable when you are dealing with a living organism like the church, because living things resist control. Consider a potted plant. In a small pot, the plant will grow until it reaches the limitations of its container. Once it feels the constraint of the pot at its roots, it stops growing. Something similar happens in the church as well, but it is often masked by numeric growth. The measure of success in shepherding God's people can never be limited to a numeric increase. Rather, maturity and multiplication constitute the growth to which the church is called, and such development can only occur when all the members of the church are using their gifts and working together toward this goal (Eph. 4:1–16). Like a small pot constricts a plant, high levels of central control stunt growth because the church cannot follow the movement of the Spirit.

Returning to the previous diagram, we see that a diminishing demand for a controlled brand and a standardized church experience leaves more dollars for the particular locations or churches in multisite and multichurch models. For example, in a minimally controlled cooperative model, a low percentage of money goes to central staff and operations, while a high percentage goes to the staff and ministry "in the trenches." This is consistent with one of our maxims: multichurch exists for its churches. Funding the multiple cooperating churches increases their responsibility, which in turn breeds ownership. Certainly, this model requires reducing central staff and operations, thereby reducing the services that are offered to the local church. But this cutback is often received well because of the valuable increase in empowerment, contextualization, and freedom in the cooperating churches.

What multichurch staffing and operations should be funded centrally? We believe that some functions benefit from reducing redundancy and seeking efficiency because they do not exert a significant effect on ownership. However, the financial framework of multichurch models is designed *to force* role and function redundancy in some areas. While redundancy slightly increases the cost for the multiple churches, if it does not take advantage of every opportunity for efficiency, then it is sometimes preferable to promote ownership and responsibility within these churches.

An example of this is printing. A federation model church has one large printer housed at its central office. Positively, pooling resources results in efficient printer use for the church as a whole. Negatively, all printing needs to be done at the one location, requiring additional central staff and volunteers to print and distribute the print jobs to the various locations with increased technical communication from the locations. Overall, this is a cheaper option for printing, but it focuses more dollars centrally. If a federation model church transitions to a cooperative model, then the church faces a choice: continue with centralized printing, thus containing costs and maintaining efficiency, or distribute this responsibility to each of the cooperating churches. Importantly, the cost to lease several smaller printers is more than the cost for one large printer; however, the additional central staffing dollars are not passed down to the cooperating churches. Despite the inefficiency for the church as a whole, the churches benefit. In cases like this, the multichurch model prefers empowerment with inefficiency to overall cost savings with efficiency.

Don't fall for the myth of control.

Myth #3: The Myth of Arrival

A third myth that needs to be exposed is that *a church will eventually get its hands around its finances, governance, and organization* and thus achieve a lasting success. When I (Brad) first arrived at Sojourn, the church had just finished three years of expansion from one church with multiple services to a church with four locations. Such growth was extremely quick and the effects were evident. Sojourn was a church of 3,500 people that was run like a church of 800. It was slow to grasp the implications of being a quickly expanded multisite church and was simultaneously trying to restructure the systems and master the finances to work within this new reality. The leadership decided to curb the impulse for more growth until the church was organized and financially stable. The myth was thinking that Sojourn could take some time to get its hands around its finances, governance, and organization. Then, once that was under control, it would be able to consider new opportunities for multiplication.

At that time, Sojourn operated under the federation model. It took the better part of two years to revamp most of our central policies and procedures to reflect this new multisite model. As this restructuring neared completion, the implication of the financial model for the four locations became strikingly clear. The federation model had a fatal flaw. If Sojourn remained on its current trajectory, its days of launching new Sojourn congregations in Louisville would be over. A misunderstanding of the implications of the multisite model had allowed the church to expand very quickly, and the relative newness of the model afforded a few years during which the leadership teams at the four locations were content with the financial model. But as the leaders and congregations matured and overcame the throes of confusion due to the newness of their ministry, their satisfaction with this structure waned. The heavy central cost of the federation model imposed severe limitations on the growth that the locations could experience. Specifically, this central financial burden caused a lack of funds for future multiplication. The myth of arrival meant that while Sojourn was waiting for things to settle down, the edges were starving. The local churches were incapable of storing up further expansion funds without a miracle or another transition.

Don't fall for the myth of arrival.

Myth #4: The Myth of Edge Growth

This situation was particularly disconcerting from a multiplication perspective because of a fourth myth: *the growth of multisite churches only occurs in new locations.* More specifically, the myth is that multisite locations reach a growth barrier within a few years, and if the church wants to continue to expand, it must start more locations. Sojourn was locked into a centralized structure that prevented it from launching new locations, and facing the possibility of no longer reaching into new areas with the gospel was devastating.

Unwilling to accept this prognostication, we began to question the myth. Is it true that multisite locations hit a barrier and thus stop growing after a couple of years? We studied various franchise and federation multisite models and saw a pattern emerge: multisite locations consistently feel underresourced. They are staffed for survival, not growth, largely due to the myth of efficiency and lowered costs. For example, a pillar or gallery model church will launch its first additional location with a bare-bones staff: a lead pastor and a part-time worship leader, who pull off Sunday services and maybe some community groups. As the location experiences growth, the size of the staff usually lags behind. Because of the high tax paid to the central organization, the location cannot be staffed for growth and soon hits a ceiling—a growth barrier—quicker than it should. The limit of growth is not a function of multisite models in general, but a function of highly centralized models.

Because of a conviction about spreading the gospel, multichurch model churches should not sacrifice the opportunity for growth at their cooperating or collective churches for the opportunity to expand the church as a whole. Rather, both opportunities are highly valued—the growth of each church and the expansion of the whole church to reach more of the city. But the cost of shifting to this model can be high. Sojourn Church made this happen by reducing the cost of central functions and moving to a cooperative multichurch model. This transition called for an immediate shift of 14 percent of its central budget—roughly $700,000—to the budgets of its four cooperating churches. These changes prompted these churches to staff for growth while producing savings for new projects and future church expansion.[3]

Don't fall for the myth of edge growth.

Four myths: The myth of efficiency and lowered costs. The myth of control and financial savings. The myth of arrival. The myth of edge growth. We have exposed and exploded these four myths about multisite models and finances, and we have narrated some of Sojourn's transition from a multisite model to a multichurch model. But before we offer a financial framework for multichurch models, we present an important principle about ownership and moral choice within these models.

Ownership and Moral Choice

The shift to a financial model that removes dollars from a centralized structure and puts them into the hands of churches on the edge is life changing for the multisite movement. It fosters a healthy distribution of power and puts resources where they can best facilitate the mission of God. It encourages ownership and fosters contextualization. It promotes maturity and multiplication.

At the same time, this movement from multisite to multichurch creates a few dilemmas of its own. While the multichurch model requires the church to reprioritize what matters, how much it matters, and when it matters, it does not reduce the (rightful) desire to support productive ministries both internally and externally. The reduction of centralized functions does limit the church's ability to invest in such ministries from a central fund. In so doing, the cooperating or collective churches support such ministries not out of obligation but because of a moral choice. In other words, in multisite models with highly centralized control, the central leadership decides which ministries to support and consequently spends central dollars received from the various locations. These may be arts, mercy, college, or any number of other ministries. Thus, the locations are obligated to support the ministries that the central leadership decides to fund. And frequently they do not have any particular connection with those ministries.

By contrast, in a multichurch model, the cooperating or collective churches communally control a majority of the overall budget—between 75 and 85 percent. The surplus is located in these churches, whose leadership teams decide how these extra funds are spent. In cases where the same ministries—arts, mercy, college—are available from the multichurch, it is the prerogative of the local churches to support them. They are given the choice. While this creates another level of responsibility for the individual churches, it fosters ownership for that ministry that mere obligation does not. As those churches decide to support the arts ministry, for example, their investment is far more than financial. When they morally choose to promote a mercy ministry, their support becomes far more than monetary. They become relationally and emotionally invested in ways that foster more passion, people, and prayer for that particular ministry.

Take international missions as another example. In multisite models, it is common for all the locations give dollars to a global program. They feel good about meeting their obligation to international missions and may even enjoy an occasional update. In multichurch models, missional engagement is a personal investment. When a cooperating or collective church sends six of its own members to the mission field and invests specifically in that ministry, there is significantly more ownership—relational, emotional, and prayerful. Members want to see where their money is going. They want to believe in the investment. By moving discretionary dollars into the hands of their churches, multichurch models increase the buy in for ministries that the churches morally decide to support.

Making Sound Financial Decisions

Finally, the essence of the financial framework of multichurch models is this: the amount of resources dedicated to central functions must be reduced or limited to the essentials. There is no magic formula; rather, each multichurch must decide individually as it takes a hard look at what is needed to promote its global vision, foster a collaborative environment, and ensure efficient operations. These three general categories determine the multichurch's essential central costs and the funds that are distributed to its multiple churches. A reasonable goal would be to reduce central costs, minimally, to less than a third of the overall budget and, ideally, to under a quarter. Think of it like a healthy family budget that commits less than a third of expenditures to the mortgage. Any more than that percentage and you could be considered "house poor." Understanding and refusing to be duped by myths exposed in this chapter will aid in the process. Additionally, the three maxims discussed earlier—multichurch exists for its churches, everything cannot matter, and multiplication is nonnegotiable—can help provide the boundaries to make sound decisions.

10

MultiMembership

Among the many issues that multichurches need to evaluate—finances, governance, leadership—one of the most significant and often overlooked elements is membership. What does it mean to be a member of a multichurch? How do members live out the reality of unity and collaboration we have been discussing? Are there any benefits the multichurch structure provides for members? Can a sense of relationship between members in one congregation and members in another congregation—or even multiple congregations—be sustained and developed?

We begin with two clear benefits of multichurch membership, followed by a discussion of multichurch's provision of specialization in ministry and extensive resources. Then we look at three benefits of the particular environment—the local church expression within the multichurch structure. Members identify with both the larger church and the specific congregation to which they belong. We will look at both of these. Finally, we offer two suggestions for how multichurch members can best experience a sense of connectedness with members of other congregations and, ultimately, with the larger church body.

A Favorable Environment

In chapter 5, we examined the idea of biodiversity and how an ecosystem's health can be measured by the amount of biodiversity present in the system. When a person cultivates an ecosystem, such as a garden or greenhouse, she develops this biodiversity by providing fertile soil and attending to the unique conditions preferred by the plants being grown. Borrowing from this idea, we start by looking at some of the ways that multichurch benefits members by providing forms of biodiversity—unique conditions and fertile soil—to encourage spiritual growth. A multichurch fosters a favorable environment for maturity and multiplication.

Spiritual Biodiversity

Multichurches are committed to a wide range of core values and diverse ministries. These elements include some or all of the following:

- gospel-centeredness
- the preaching/teaching of Scripture
- prayer
- worship
- sound theology
- discipleship
- Spirit-endowed and -empowered missional engagement and multiplication
- mercy
- celebration of the ordinances of baptism and the Lord's Supper
- giving to support pastors and the poor
- care and counseling
- education
- the promotion of covenantal community characterized by faith, hope, and love

Because a multichurch encourages a biblically promoted breadth of ministry, it is inherently nonreductionistic. It refuses to commit the common error of many evangelical churches, focusing on some but not all of these biblically endorsed values and ministries.

Reductionism is everywhere. One church might be known for its worship and preaching. It exists for the glory of God alone. Another church concentrates on discipleship, being committed to the growth and health of its members. Still another church focuses on reaching the lost through evangelism and missions. It is the "Great Commission church."

While worship, discipleship, and missional engagement are essential elements of the church, and a church's commitment to those elements is right and admirable, reducing the church to one or a few of those elements illegitimately diminishes what the church is and does. Sadly, it is a natural tendency within the organization of the church to concentrate on some ministries to the neglect of others. While we can never fully avoid this problem, the multichurch structure is a helpful corrective to this trend. A multichurch is committed from the beginning to the full expression of biblically promoted values and ministries. This has two benefits for members. It provides many opportunities for them to use their gifts within the body, and it enhances the accessibility of the church.

First, because of its commitment to avoid reductionism, a multichurch is marked by a wide diversity of ministries and opportunities for people to use their gifts. Rather than limiting what the church values or encourages, a multichurch invites its members to explore their gifts and passions with the freedom to use them for the advancement of the kingdom of God.

Imagine a church member who has a passion for international missions but attends a church that focuses exclusively on the Sunday service, small groups, Sunday school, and workplace evangelism. This member struggles to apply her passion for cross-cultural, international ministry to the opportunities that fit the vision of her church. Certainly, she may conform to the opportunities available and may be satisfied. More often, however, she has to look outside her church for opportunities to use her gifts, seeking out parachurch organizations to assist her in pursuing her passion. A multichurch, by contrast, maintains a commitment to a breadth of ministry and offers more opportunities for its members. She finds her niche within her church family through short-term missions opportunities, participation in missions school, or even packing up everything and becoming a missionary.

The second benefit of the multichurch structure is accessibility (i.e., wide availability to others). A multichurch values being mission-oriented and exists to reach its city by establishing multiple congregations in various neighborhoods. Because of that, church members who engage non-Christian family members, friends, colleagues, and other acquaintances with the gospel and lead them to Christ do not have to coax these new believers to travel twenty-five minutes to a pillar church. Instead, the new believers can become part of the neighborhood congregation located six minutes from their home. This localized environment fosters neighborhood missional endeavors—members reaching nonbelievers in their context and keeping them engaged with the community there, in order to reach even more people with the good news. Nothing is more encouraging than to hear stories of a member of the church reaching out to someone at work and see another church member reaching the same person in their neighborhood.

Multichurch discipleship provides another example of accessibility. Because there are multiple congregations, most discipleship will be "cultivated" geographically. Community groups or missional communities are typically congregation-specific and meet together in geographic proximity. Because of this, multichurch community is rooted in both relationship and location, and discipleship is fostered by relational and spatial proximity.

These cooperative missional and discipleship ministries can lead to some interesting and exciting results. Emma, who is active in one congregation, shares the gospel with her cousin Courtney, who lives in the same city but in a neighborhood distant from Emma. Courtney has questions about the gospel and eventually becomes a Christian. With a multichurch, she can be connected with the same church but in a location close to where she lives and works. Courtney shares in the same church identity as her cousin, but she does not have to be completely dependent on Emma for her follow-up and discipleship. Emma can encourage Courtney in discipleship, as Courtney becomes active in that other congregation. This is what we mean when we say that multichurch makes the body of Christ *accessible*. A single church is shared by multiple members who belong to diverse congregations. There is shared identity and ministry, but it is not bound by geographic limitations.

Thus, a multichurch promotes spiritual diversity by which members have many opportunities to use their gifts, and the accessibility of the church is enhanced.

Unique Conditions

Although multichurch is committed to a wide range of core values and essential ministries (thus avoiding reductionism), ministry is also specialized. Returning to our gardening analogy, if you adjust conditions such as the amount of water and direct sunlight, you control the health of particular plants. By recognizing that each plant thrives in different conditions, you establish the best range of conditions within a single ecosystem that foster biodiversity. In a multichurch, this is characterized by developing conditions that encourage growth broadly and deeply. While all the congregations of a multichurch engage in some of the ministry elements (preaching, baptism, the Lord's Supper, discipleship, and multiplication, for example), other elements will be emphasized in some of the congregations—but not all of them.

What does this look like, practically? Consider a multichurch that is dedicated to mercy. It exists to extend concrete, compassionate help to the poor and marginalized. This includes former convicts, prostitutes, the unemployed, the handicapped, and others on the fringes of society. Some of the congregations of this multichurch are located in neighborhoods where there is a large concentration of these disenfranchised groups. Other congregations exist in locations where the marginalized are less concentrated or, perhaps, nearly nonexistent. This does not mean that the people in those advantaged locations lack the need for mercy ministries, but the expression of mercy has a different form in those neighborhoods or contexts. This multichurch does not need to have a mercy ministry meeting the same need in each of its congregations. Rather, it can concentrate its merciful endeavors in the locations most in need, with the congregations in those neighborhoods focusing on mercy ministries that fit the needs of their community.

The multichurch as a whole obeys the biblical directive to be merciful and engages in concrete works of mercy through particular congregations. Because all the members of the multichurch have the opportunity to contribute through their giving to these mercy ministries, all of them have a part in extending concrete, compassionate help to those in need. Although members at one congregation may not be directly involved in working with the unemployed or aiding in community development, they support such merciful actions through their giving. Additionally, as members in advantaged locations want to get involved in more direct ways, they have well-functioning mercy ministries in different neighborhoods through which to work. They can serve meals to the women in sex clubs, help the unemployed with resume writing and job training, or offer microloans to the poor to start businesses, all through their church. Multichurch promotes extensiveness and intensiveness in values and ministries, and members flourish in this nonreductionistic, specialized environment.

Fertile Soil

Involvement in a congregation that is part of a larger whole provides members with extensive resources. This is akin to having fertile soil in which to grow different kinds of plants. When you have fertile soil and add a variety of nutrients, water, sunlight, and space to grow, the result is a healthy garden. In a similar way, the availability of resources promotes healthy growth within the church and among its members.

Importantly, these resources can be shared across congregations. Sound theology, solid leaders, a compelling vision, a centralized administration, pastoral care, many opportunities for leadership development, and other "nutrients" foster healthy growth in the multichurch model. Each congregation has some of these resources, as the Holy Spirit has gifted the members of the congregation. And wherever a congregation lacks, the resources of the larger whole—the multichurch—are available.

If one congregation has a concentration of counselors, they can make themselves available to help the other congregations with pastoral care. If one congregation has a concentration of missions experts, they can host a school of missions at their location, thus making that training available to the other congregations. If one congregation has a concentration of people who excel at developing children's ministries, those specialists can make their expertise available to the other congregations.

On a regular basis, the local church pastors can meet during the week to pray, study together, suggest preaching outlines and key points that can be made in their sermons, encourage one another, and debrief their sermons from the preceding week. If the congregations use a common liturgy for the Sunday worship service, the worship leaders can meet together to develop the liturgy for the upcoming gathering. Multichurch fosters the development of members by providing healthy environments that promote opportunities, accessibility, specialization, and the sharing of resources.

A Particular Environment

Within a large garden, it is advantageous to construct specific areas with unique conditions preferred by specific plants. In other words, if you want biodiversity, you cannot take a one-size-fits-all approach. To this point, we have looked at the benefits that the multichurch structure brings to members because the individual congregations are united to a central church identity. But what about the benefits that members enjoy from being part of a particular environment—a specific congregation—within a multichurch? And how do you develop a sense of identity and belonging between members active in one congregation and members active in another congregation—even multiple congregations? How do you avoid isolation, division, and churches pursuing their own local mission without regard for the larger body?

Communication of your identity as a church is key. Multichurch members identify themselves as being a part of one church made up of multiple interdependent or independent congregations, yet their primary identity is always with their particular congregation. It is with that congregation that they worship, engage in close community, serve, grow, and live missionally. There are three benefits for members that flow from their primary identification being with their particular congregation: they are connected to other local members, they have a sense of personal connection to the elders, and they have access to local opportunities for leadership development.

Membership

Although a multichurch has one united membership, both entrance into and exclusion from church membership is the responsibility of a particular congregation. New people go through the membership process at a particular congregation. There is no "generic" sense of belonging apart from participation in a local congregation. To become a member, you need to first apply. Afterwards, you are interviewed for membership, and finally, you are accepted for membership through that particular congregation's process.

Members become part of a family. Culturally, the idea of membership has lost much of its power. You can become a "member" of your grocery store, your gas station, and your favorite sub shop, as well as your bank, gym, and neighborhood pool. This equates membership with coupons and skipping workouts. But membership in a family is different. Family membership obligates members to one another in the best sense of the word. The church should mirror the home with its members as brothers and sisters obligated to one another through the bond of love.

The benefits of family membership include all the joys of life together and support for challenging moments. These difficult moments include helping one another walk with Christ and resist sin. On the regretful occasion when a member becomes entrenched in sin, the community is compelled by love to draw them back to Jesus. Such members experience church discipline through their particular church family. They go through the prescribed disciplinary steps as outlined by Jesus (Matt. 18:15–20; cf. 1 Cor. 5:1–13). They are called to repentance, reconciliation, and restitution by their brothers and sisters. If those actions do not take place, then they are asked to leave the fellowship until they are repentant through a process that is particular to their congregation.

Importantly, membership always has a reference to the larger whole. New people become members of the multichurch, even though the process of membership operates through a particular congregation. In cases of church discipline, it is especially important that all the congregations communicate to enhance care for those who have been sinned against and to increase the chances of reconciliation. This also prevents people from avoiding repentance by inserting themselves into another congregation.

The members of a multichurch gain from being part of a larger whole: hundreds, perhaps thousands, of multichurch members transforming their city through the gospel. The members benefit from identifying with their particular congregation, which bears the responsibility for both receiving new members and caring for them.

Eldership

Like its membership, a multichurch has a unified eldership, while its members are under the supervision and care of the elders of their particular congregation. This intercepts the complaint that some have made of multisite models whose elders are the leaders of the larger whole but not of any member in particular. Critics might ask, "How is Hebrews 13:17 actualized in a setting where elders form a central leadership body?" Hebrews 13:17 is written to church members: "Obey your leaders and submit to them, for they are keeping watch over your souls, as those who will have to give an account. Let them do this with joy and not with groaning, for that would be of no advantage to you" (ESV).

In a multichurch setting, the application is relatively straightforward. Members follow the leadership of their congregational elders, who bear the responsibility to teach, pray for, disciple, and shepherd the members entrusted to them. These elders will give an account to the Lord for the members of their congregation. The full council of elders will also give an account for the multichurch as a whole. So there is both local accountability at the member level and collective responsibility among the elders at the central level. In either case the actualization of Hebrews 13:17 is not problematic. Members are directly under the care and supervision of the elders of their congregation. Because those elders are part of and in unity with the full council of elders, the multichurch is under the unified governance and management of that council. With wisdom, prayer, and vision, the full council of elders teaches and leads the larger whole.

Again, we see that members of a multichurch gain from being part of a larger whole: the full council of elders leading hundreds, perhaps thousands, of members in transforming their city through the gospel. In addition, members benefit from identifying with their particular congregation, whose elders bear the responsibility for leading, teaching, praying for, and shepherding them.

Leadership Development

By now it should be obvious that the multichurch model is committed to constant leadership development. Members of a multichurch are equipped to lead and minister through their particular congregation's leadership development process. This process of identification, assessment, and development takes place within each local congregation. Foundational and core ministry leaders from the local churches often collaborate to standardize assessment and development, making it easier for leaders to cross-train and transition between churches. In addition to this standardized training, local leaders also contextualize the training for their congregation and are responsible for any additional development and equipping they have the resources to employ. In this way leaders are developed within a specific ministry context, even if they move to a leadership position that benefits the multichurch as a whole.

Vincent, a university student, recently became a new member of a multichurch. He joined a community group where he was discipled, cared for, and involved in service in that community. Soon he became an apprentice of the community group leader, a process that called for him to be trained to multiply a new community group. As he proved himself capable of leading his own group, Vincent launched a new group with a half dozen members. Through discipleship, care, and involving the other members in the mission—including the training of an apprentice and the expansion of his group—Vincent arrived at a point where the community group multiplied and his new apprentice started a new group.

As these groups expanded and multiplied, Vincent became a neighborhood leader responsible for coaching the leaders of the community groups that have multiplied from his original group. And as he continues to mature and develops the character and competencies as outlined in 1 Timothy 3:1–7, he will eventually become an elder. While he continues to be responsible for the leadership development of community groups at his particular congregation, Vincent is now part of the full council of elders helping with leadership development for the whole church.

As he develops even further, he might become the lead pastor of a new congregation or he may leave to plant a new church in another city.

As you can see, members of a multichurch gain from being part of a larger whole that is committed to and in need of leadership development. The multichurch model provides significantly more leadership roles for people to be involved in, which in turn allows members to develop the leadership skills to rise to the level of their calling. In some cases, this leadership development results in new leaders being prepared for responsibility for the whole multichurch. Members benefit from identifying with their particular congregation, which provides many of the aspects of leadership development, including the identification of potential leaders, basic and advanced training, ongoing assessment, and advancement for proven leaders.

A United Environment

Up to this point, we have emphasized the benefits of members being connected to particular congregations while still part of a larger whole. However, this can sometimes work against unity in the church. There may be times when members identify with local congregations against other congregations, or congregations see themselves as being in competition with one another. How can a sense of unity and healthy relationship be sustained and developed? We have two suggestions toward that end.

First, in keeping with the multichurch pattern exhibited by the early church, a multichurch should seek to periodically gather together as a whole. This united gathering can take various forms. One option is to have all members gather together for a quarterly meeting that might include a worship service with the celebration of baptism and the Lord's Supper. This could be a congregational meeting in which the business of the whole church is carried out along with any exercise of church discipline. Another option is to have all members gather together for special days in the liturgical year such as Christmas Eve, Ash Wednesday, Good Friday, Easter Sunday, Ascension Sunday, Pentecost Sunday, and/ or Trinity Sunday.

Of course, the larger a multichurch grows, the harder it is to find a place where all its members can gather together. There may be space restrictions, including the cost of renting a venue large enough to accommodate all the participants. There is also the difficulty of scheduling a time when everyone can meet, among other logistical matters (e.g., rooms for nursing mothers and programs for young children). Still, large multichurches can budget for these details if they are committed to gathering together (and we strongly urge that they do, in accordance with the biblical pattern).

Second, in keeping with this pattern, it is essential for a multichurch to operate as interdependent or collaborating congregations of one church. While members most often gather in their particular congregations, connectedness between the congregations can be fostered through regular communication among them. For example, video presentations of what is going on in the other locations can be regularly scheduled as part of worship services, community groups, and congregational meetings. Representatives from other locations can give live updates about what is happening with their congregation. The lead pastors can engage in pulpit exchange and preach in other congregational worship services. And at united gatherings, each of the lead pastors can provide an update from his congregation so the church shares in the joys and challenges of ministry together.

Another way to cultivate unity is to host regular congregational meetings—monthly, quarterly, or annually—for the members of each particular congregation, in which the leaders reemphasize the multichurch's vision, explain plans for expansion, and highlight current joys and challenges. These meetings can also be used to tell stories about what is happening at the other congregations, so they help to cultivate a sense that each congregation is part of a larger whole.

A multichurch always straddles these two realities: the larger whole and the particular congregations. Unity exists at both levels, and it takes creative thinking to best promote that united environment. When it is done well, a multichurch can foster a sense of connectedness among the members of its multiple congregations and, ultimately, with the larger whole.

Membership in a Multichurch

In this chapter as we have looked at meaningful membership in a multichurch, we have explored three key points. First, we emphasized the favorable environment of a multichurch. People active in a multichurch are members of a particular congregation and the larger whole. A multichurch is nonreductionistic, specialized, and resourceful, and it offers the benefits of opportunities for members to use their gifts through enhanced accessibility.

Second, we highlighted the particular environment of a multichurch. People active in a multichurch are members of a specific congregation. While identifying themselves as being a part of one church made up of several congregations, their primary identity is with the particular congregation where they worship, engage in close community, serve, grow, and live missionally. Because of this particular identification, members experience the benefits related to membership, eldership, and leadership development.

Third, we underscored the united environment of a multichurch. People active in a multichurch are members of one another. Because of this unity, the multichurch needs to work hard so the members of a particular congregation can experience a sense of connectedness with members of the other congregations and, ultimately, with the larger whole.

SECTION 3

SETTING OUT

I'm sure the feeling of fear, as long as you can take advantage
of it and not be rendered useless by it, can make you extend
yourself beyond what you would regard as your capacity. If
you're afraid, the blood seems to flow freely through the veins,
and you really do feel a sense of stimulation.

SIR EDMUND HILLARY

Martin Luther King Jr. said, "Faith is taking the first step even when
you don't see the whole staircase." After all that we have laid out in the
first two sections, it still takes a tremendous leap of faith to leave what
is comfortable and known, and propel your church into the unknown
world of multichurch ministry. You will need to press into the love of God
and trust that he is faithful to his church. This final section of the book
provides some lessons for transitioning your church into a multichurch
and includes the rest of the story of Sojourn Community Church. While
some of what we have said in this book may sound nice in theory, our
goal in this section is to show you the practical challenges of initiating
meaningful change. In chapter 1, we shared some of the mistakes and
lessons we have learned in our experience at Sojourn. This final section

focuses on how we led the transformation from a federation multisite model church to a cooperative multichurch model church. It is an example of at least one church that has gone on the expedition ahead of you . . . and made it back alive.

11

Navigating Transition

Perhaps you are considering the crucial step of navigating your church through a transition to a new model. You may pastor an existing multisite church, or you may simply be interested in the multisite model and hope to cast a vision for a healthy and sustainable model of multisite ministry— this new model we are calling multichurch. Leading people through change is a difficult task, so you will need wisdom and a clear vision of where you want to go. In this chapter, we will prepare you for this process by presenting four steps in the navigation phase: scouting the terrain, charting a course, starting the journey, and rerouting if necessary. We will conclude this chapter on transitioning to multichurch with three final lessons: avoiding communication degradation, working with slow adopters, and leading in the Spirit.

Leading through Change

I (Brad) have four children, and almost every day, my wife and I lament how fast they are growing up. The other day, my wife asked our youngest if he would please stop growing. He happily agreed to stay four forever. Of course, we were joking. It's a cute sentiment—but the reality of a perpetual four-year-old would be devastating. We love this age, but one of the joys of parenting is watching him grow, learn new things, and mature into adulthood. If our son were to stop growing and changing, it would be a tragedy. We would never be able to talk as peers or watch his children—our grandchildren—play.

The desire to keep things as they are is called sentimentality. Unfortunately, it is rampant in the church. A church experiences amazing moments—conducting its first worship service, celebrating baptisms, breaking ground on a new building, seeing new believers grow into maturity, and starting a new church. These wonderful and life-changing moments eventually establish themselves as "the good ol' days." A decade passes and the church changes. Some of those who've been around since the beginning now long for those days. "Remember when . . . ?"

The problem is that this nostalgia forgets the messy details. We have a tendency to edit out the challenges and the mistakes and problems that we inevitably had to deal with during those "good ol' days." We forget the hard work required to get where we are today.[1] Some of the members who look at the past with fondness do so because they were not involved in those problems. They were not in the trenches during the moments of anxiety and stress, when the leaders were just trying to hold it all together. So these members often pine for the past while the church advances.

They may even want the church to stop growing. But growth is a wonderful thing. A church that stops growing is a tragedy. This is not to say that a church must always grow *numerically*, although we hope and pray that new people are continually added to Christ's body. Numerical growth is only *one* measure of health. Growth should also be experienced and measured in maturity and mission. But as we argued earlier, living things grow—indeed, they must. And growth necessitates change.

Yet, people perceive growth as good and change as bad. Why? Because they often view change through the lens of what will be lost.

One of the most thoughtful works on preparing for and leading change is *Leadership on the Line*.[2] Authors Ronald Heifetz and Marty Linsky identify two categories of challenges that require organizational change: technical and adaptive. Technical challenges are problems that the organization has "the necessary know-how and procedures" to handle.[3] Adaptive challenges "require experiments, new discoveries, and adjustment from numerous places in the organization or community. For adaptive change, people must learn new ways—changing attitudes, values, and behaviors—to make the leap necessary to thrive in the new environment."[4]

This distinction is helpful because the transition to a multichurch model necessitates both technical and adaptive changes. New structures and procedures may present technical challenges, of course, and those must be addressed. But the transition to being one church made of interdependent churches or one church uniting independent churches also requires changing attitudes, values, and behaviors. As Heifetz and Linsky warn, "Habits, values, and attitudes, even dysfunctional ones, are part of one's identity. To change the way people see and do things is to challenge how they define themselves."[5]

This is why transitions like a shift to multisite or multichurch models stir up so much resistance. People have a hard time giving up what they know for the unknown, regardless of how promising that possibility may be. When the people of Israel were wandering in the dessert, they longed to return to Egypt. Why would they want to return to slavery? It sounds crazy! But Egypt was familiar, and they knew there was food. At least there, they got fed. They remembered their enslavement as being more comfortable than the freedom of living in the wilderness. They had to reprogram their habits, values, and attitudes to align with the glorious hope of the promised land ahead of them. So it should come as no surprise to church leaders that when they attempt to introduce constructive change, they end up facing significant resistance, even when the change is for the church's good.

Our point here is not to discourage your church from making the transition to multichurch, but to help leaders prepare adequately for the challenges of this change. The people of Israel longed for the familiarity of slavery, but they were far better off remaining in the desert with God in hope of one day experiencing life in the promised land. Despite their present discomfort, the change was worth the pain, as Moses and the others led them through the wilderness.

The Process of Change

The process of change will be unique to each congregation, and there is ample advice on how to orchestrate change within an organization.[6]

Our goal here is not to retrace what others have said. Instead, we offer a simple framework with which to start and which can be modified for each church's particular situation. Throughout this book, we compare this transition to an expedition toward a new and promising destination. To reach the destination, four steps are necessary. You must

1. scout the terrain,
2. chart a course,
3. start the journey, and
4. reroute as necessary.

The process of change in most organizations—from the military to businesses to educational institutions—uses some iteration of these four steps. These are not original to us, and other approaches may be used if they are a better fit for your culture and context.

Step 1: Scout the Terrain

Expeditions that end in tragedy often fail at the start by not accurately scouting the terrain. For our context, a church about to embark on the journey into multichurch should not begin the process until it has done a thorough examination of its readiness to execute the transition. It is vitally important that the church be prepared. This preparation must happen with reference to its convictions, organization, and finances.

Convictional Preparation

To successfully transition to a multichurch model, a church must have unity in both theological and philosophical convictions. The theological convictions in chapter 5 and the philosophical convictions in section 2 provide the foundation for this transition. In *Start with Why*, Simon Sinek explains the importance of having a convictional foundation: "People don't buy WHAT you do; they buy why you do it."[7] For a church transitioning governments and leadership structures, it is essential for the leaders, staff, and church members to be on the same page. Everyone must take ownership of the change. Simply shifting your processes and polity is not inspiring and will lead to resistance. Ensure that the whole church understands the "why" behind the transition.

Before you begin a transition to a multisite or multichurch model, take time to assess the unity of the church—especially your leadership team—to get a sense of its theological and philosophical convictions. Take time to get on the same page by working through chapters 5–9. This can save your church plenty of headaches down the road. Discuss the following questions with your leaders:

- Do we have theological and philosophical alignment in order to transition to a multichurch model?
- Are our convictions prompting us to employ a multichurch methodology?
- What values, ideals, sacred cows, and other convictions will be affected by the change to multichurch?

Organizational Preparation

After an evaluation of convictional readiness, the church must assess its organizational preparedness. Chapter 6 presents two charts—the conviction-urgency chart, and the conviction-ability chart—for evaluating the church organizationally in terms of what matters, how much it matters, and when it matters. Working through these charts should give a church a clear understanding of the urgency with which to pursue transition to a multichurch model. The goal is to make sure that the church's processes, policies, and organizational behaviors align with its convictions. Be warned: as a church clarifies its convictions, it may be embarrassed to discover how far out of line these are with its practice of ministry. Another goal of this preparation is to discern the impact that a multichurch structure will have on the church as a whole. Assessing structures, policies, and the pulse of the people enables a church to determine its ability to transition to this new model and how urgently the transition needs to take place.

In the bestselling book *Good to Great*, Jim Collins explains that an organization must "*first* [get] the right people on the bus (and the wrong people off the bus) and *then* figure out where to drive it."[8] This is sound advice because structures and policies are easier to change than people. In the transition to multichurch, getting the right leadership and staff will make changes to structures and policies much easier to address. But knowing what to do and actually doing it are two different things! Getting the right people can be difficult because the church's leadership and staff have been built on another set of convictions—those of the current model. Transitioning this same team of people is a challenge because the new model of multichurch requires a greater amount of responsibility, ownership, and contextualization.

Allow us to share an example of what we mean. One of the struggles Sojourn faced during our transition to the cooperative model was patience. We needed patience *not* to move forward until we were ready, and this willingness to wait was a major point of contention among the leadership team. Our new structure would require our current elders and staff to exercise more authority than they did in the old model, yet the leaders felt we were moving too slowly. In tension with moving faster was our sense that these elders and staff needed time to grow into their new responsibilities. In the midst of these disagreements, there was the potential to paralyze the church.

During this time, one of our pastors shared a helpful example from his life as a father. He said his children would never have learned to pour milk if he was unwilling to clean up some messes. He wasn't being condescending; he was encouraging us to give our leaders and staff, as well as ourselves, opportunity to grow. In other words, one of the keys to our success as a church would be to cultivate a culture of failure. As we have discussed, multichurch requires a culture that not only allows for failure but actually celebrates the willingness to attempt great things. This reminded us all that organizational readiness does not require that everyone demonstrates competence in a new role. Readiness is a measure of the willingness of the church to accept the limitations of its leaders and staff as they grow into their new responsibilities.

Some church leaders and staff may resist change for convictional reasons, and in these cases, you will need to decide if you can guide them through the transition or if it is better for them to simply move on. Accepting the "casualties" of change is difficult, but it is necessary for the health of the church overall ... and for the people who would not thrive in the new model. We will return to this point later in the chapter.

With this in mind, be sure you work through chapter 6 to assess your church's organizational readiness *before* you begin to implement a transition. Be sure to ask these primary questions:

- What organizational structures and policies will be affected by the transition to multichurch, and how should we change them?
- What will be the schedule for the transition of authority and transfer of responsibility?
- Do we have the right people to make the transition?
- If some leaders and staff are not currently ready for the transition, are they able to grow into their new responsibilities?
- For leaders and staff who are not ready, can we prepare them for their new responsibilities, or do they need to be released?
- How will the transition affect the current ministries of the church?

Financial Preparation

Managing a crisis, especially one that involves money, is never enjoyable. Therefore, it is important to get the church's financial house in order *before* beginning the change process. Multichurch should never be viewed as a "Hail Mary" strategy to help get the church financially into the black. Conviction—not pragmatism—should lead the way forward. The church should establish a clear financial plan before it transitions to multichurch in order to prevent the chaos of simultaneously changing its structure, polity, and finances. Assess the church's financial position beginning with a review of the myths we covered in chapter 9, and be sure to understand clearly what multichurch provides and does not provide from a financial standpoint.

In addition, you will need to understand how the transition to multichurch entails a redistribution of decision-making power. This redistribution carries with it inherent risk as more people are making decisions about—and spending—money. You must have the adequate cash reserves to cover unforeseen expenses associated with the transition. Moreover, the redistribution of spending authority can create confusion regarding budgets and the parties responsible for them. Assessing the church's financial readiness should include implementing a system of reporting to handle the new budgeting structure. This is a key reason why core financial functions should remain centralized in the multichurch model. This guarantees some financial accountability and stability for the church.

So before you implement a transition plan to multichurch, be sure to assess the church's financial readiness by working through chapter 9. To be specific, ask the following primary questions:

- Is the church ready to transition to a multichurch model without running undue financial risk?
- What will be the financial effect of the transition on leaders, staff, and congregations?
- What is the church's system for budgeting, financial reporting, and other money matters in the new structure?

Convictional readiness. Organizational readiness. Financial readiness. It is vitally important that your church is prepared in these three areas to complete the transition to multichurch well. This is what it means to "scout the terrain."

Step 2: Chart a Course

After scouting ahead, the second step is to chart a course. Practically speaking, this means preparing a written transition plan. This written proposal sets forth the purposes, goals, changes, structures, policies, responsibilities, as well as a timeline, for the change to the new model. This written plan reduces confusion and brings clarity as the transition is communicated to the various groups in the church: pastors/elders, deacons and deaconesses, staff, and members.

Charting a course should be understood as an iterative process. As the transition advances, the plan can change, with some elements dropping out, others being modified, and still others being added. Throughout the transition, those responsible for it should communicate, communicate, communicate. They should also involve as many people in the process as appropriate in order to foster collaboration, ownership, and participation.

An important way of developing this "buy-in" is by getting feedback. The church should encourage its leaders, staff, and members, in differing degrees and ways, to speak into the plan and the process for transition. Schedule formal meetings like forums and community groups, and informal meetings between those responsible for the transition and people who want to offer suggestions and express concerns. As these people participate in the planning process, they prevent the leaders from developing a "savior complex." They also begin to own the transition, and their continued commitment to the transition helps to guarantee its success.

Eventually this "buy-in" will need to be formalized. Leaders, staff, and members will need to embrace their respective responsibilities for the transition, and commit themselves to seeing the process of transition through to the end. Moreover, they must agree to face the inevitable challenges and failures with grace and forgiveness rather than complaints and bitterness. They must pledge to withstand any waves of resistance that might arise. You may want to consider a formal vote or a special service where this commitment is made.

Charting the course puts the transition map into the hands of the church's leaders, staff, and members as they embark on the journey to multichurch.

Step 3: Start the Journey

Having scouted the terrain and charted a course, the third step is embarking on the journey. To foster ownership, the actual execution of the transition should engage as many people as appropriate. Leaders should be careful not to take shortcuts by simply dictating the changes or by taking matters into their own hands. It requires patience to allow others the time they need to adapt and learn new responsibilities. Remember to continually communicate and to celebrate the progress with the goal of empowering others—not being the hero.

As you depart on the journey, be clear about the process and schedule. For most churches, the transition from a multisite model to a multichurch model has two major components. First, there is the question of polity, or the governance structure. Second, there is the matter of the organizational framework. A healthy transition starts with the shift in polity *before* you begin organizational change. This allows for the new governing structure to speak into the new organizational framework, infusing trust into the new polity. While leading the new governing team through organizational change will require more time and energy, it is essential for the change to take place. Reversing this sequence may unintentionally communicate a lack of faith in the new team and erode the ownership of local leaders in the transition process. Because the goal is empowerment, lead with empowerment.

Step 4: Rerouting as Necessary

Finally, after scouting the terrain, charting a course, and starting the journey, you may need to make some midcourse corrections. Rarely do explorers on a journey know all the details of the terrain or chart a perfect course with an infallible map. Often, they forget to bring all the necessary supplies and need to make adjustments along the route. As the old proverb warns, "any plan that cannot change is a bad plan." As a church pursues the transition to multichurch, it needs adaptability and flexibility.

A good measure of your journey's progress is the emotional state of the church's leaders and staff. Are they confused, bitter, worn out, and despairing? Or are they enthusiastic, hopeful, energized, and joyful? Stay attentive to the transition's impact on people. This will help the church know when to pivot and when to stay the course.

Heifetz and Linsky refer to this as "getting on the balcony."[9] They explain the need to consider the activities of the organization from a different perspective, from a vantage point that sees the whole picture. It is the process of taking the pulse of the organization and learning how to manage the anxiety that people will naturally experience. My former basketball coach told us to "slow down and go faster" when our zeal was greater than our ability. Going a touch slower at times can prevent conflicts and costly mistakes. Slow down to rally the troops, to enhance collaboration, and even to change the plan and the process. Do not make the mistake of forging ahead at any cost. It will save the church time and effort in the long run.

Scout the terrain. Chart a course. Start the journey. And reroute as necessary. If you think of a transition as an expedition toward a new and promising destination, these four steps will serve you well in the transition to a multichurch model.

Final Lessons for the Journey

We conclude this chapter on transitioning to multichurch with three final lessons that will help you experience a healthy transition in your church. First, avoid communication degradation. Second, learn to work with the "slow adopters"—people who don't catch on as quickly as the rest of the church. Finally, remember to lead in the Spirit.

Communication Degradation

"All leaders must have two things: they must have a vision of the world that does not exist and they must have the ability to communicate it."[10] That second component is truly essential. Communicate, communicate, communicate! We cannot overstate the importance of communication within a changing organization. Of anything you do, communication will have the most dramatic effect—positively or negatively—on the success of the transition.

One obstacle to good communication practices is something we refer to as *communication degradation*. This is the tendency for a message to break down as it is delivered from one group to another. This degradation is pretty simple and quite common. The first team to explore a transition to multichurch tends to spend the most time scouting the terrain and charting the course (e.g., researching the cost, considering the implications of such a transition, and sequencing the transition steps). As this team makes decisions and communicates them to the second level of leaders, communicative shortcuts are taken. These shortcuts typically happen because the first team makes some assumptions. They assume that the second group has been a part of the conversation from the beginning, even though they know that is not the case. Thus, it is important to remember that the second team has some gaps in its understanding of the transition plan and process. As the plan and process gets communicated to the church staff and members, more shortcuts are taken and more assumptions are made. In addition, *communication fatigue* sets in. This is when the same message is delivered so many times that it gets broken down to soundbites and bumper sticker slogans.

One such breakdown came to my attention as I (Brad) sat down for lunch with a long-standing, and eminently secure, staff member during our transition. The first thing he wanted to know was if he still had a job. In our communication, we had failed to address issues of job security with the staff because it had been settled long before we began to communicate the plan.

To be clear, it is necessary to simplify the plan for some settings. However, during a transition, gaps in transmitting and understanding are one of the primary causes of confusion and conflict. The worry and uncertainty that church members feel are difficult to anticipate because leaders have spent so much time and effort with the transition plan that they just cannot see the pitfalls. The leaders are so saturated with the plan and the vision that they have a hard time understanding the objections. Knowing this will help you to be patient and deliberate as you communicate the transition plan and process. You need to find a balance between overcommunication that frustrates the leaders and staff who are familiar with the plan, and undercommunication that leads to confusion about the transition. As we emphasized earlier, pay attention to the impact of the transition on the leaders, staff, and members. This will go a long way toward avoiding communication degradation.

Working with Slow Adopters

What does a church do with leaders, staff, and members who are not resistant to the transition to multichurch but who take what seems like an inordinate amount of time to understand, embrace, and engage in the transition? Heifetz and Linsky give great advice for working with these slow adopters: accept responsibility for the mess, acknowledge their loss, model the behavior, and accept casualties.[11]

First, accept responsibility. Leaders in the transition to multichurch must identify and accept responsibility for their contribution to the current chaotic situation, even as the church labors to move people to a different, better place. Even more importantly, rather than developing an "us versus them" mentality, the quick adopters and slow adopters should face the problems together, with each one accepting some share of responsibility for the chaos.

Second, acknowledge the loss that people are experiencing. When a church transitions to multichurch, people are required to adapt. The forced change of attitudes, behaviors, roles, and more results in substantial loss. At stake may be a choice between two values (for example, being comfortable with what is familiar, and being missional through change leading to expansion), both of which are important to the way they understand themselves. Or it may summon people to close the distance between their espoused values and their actual behavior. Of course, this takes time, especially for slow adopters. Moreover, confronting the gap between values and behavior—exposing the internal contradictions in our lives and communities—requires going through a period of loss. Indeed, these changes often demand some disloyalty to our roots. For leaders of the transition, this challenge does not seem like much of a sacrifice. But in feeling so, they may discount the sense of loss with which others struggle, thereby failing to love and lead them properly.

Transitional leadership involves helping the church figure out what and whom it is willing to sacrifice. Of all the values honored by the community, which of them can be surrendered in the interest of progress? And why should these sacrifices be made? People are willing to suffer loss if they see the reason for it. Additionally, naming and thereby acknowledging the loss is crucial. The leaders of the transition need to let the others know that they recognize and appreciate what is being sacrificed on the way to creating a better future. Thus, explicitly acknowledging the difficulty of the change they are being asked to make, and recognizing the real value of this sacrifice, can be helpful in the transition to multichurch, especially for slow adopters.

Third, model the behavior. Beyond acknowledging the sacrifice and pain of loss that will be incurred in the transition to multichurch, leaders need to model the behavior they expect the others to exhibit. They should admit their own fears and worries, and confess the sacrifices they must make for the sake of the shift. For example, centralized leaders may need to yield significant responsibility, authority, and compensation for their global roles and accept a more limited (but not inferior) ministry in one of the cooperating or collaborative churches. They can face their own transition with courage, hope, trust, and lament, and model the behavior they are asking the others to display.

Finally, accept casualties. The church may need to release some people from their responsibilities to bring actual change in culture and structure. While such casualties are indeed difficult, they are necessary. Moreover, some slow adopters may grow weary of the sacrifices they are called to make during the transition, and therefore leave the church. In such cases it is important for leaders to avoid taking such decisions personally. Philosophical differences are not sinful. Just as Paul and Barnabas disagreed about John Mark (Acts 15:36–41), disagreeing parties can amicably part ways if proper pastoral care is provided. The goal is to keep the list of casualties small, but the church needs to accept those losses with the faith that God is leading all parties to greener pastures.

A church that transitions to a multichurch model must be prepared to work with slow adopters. By accepting responsibility for the mess, acknowledging loss, modeling the expected behavior, and accepting casualties, the hope is that in due time, the slow adopters will adjust well and flourish with the rest of the new multichurch.

Leading in the Spirit

At a gathering of a group of pastors, one of the leaders lamented that he had become "too comfortable handling sacred things."[12] In an age when the church is obsessed with performance and success, many leaders fall into this mistake. This overfamiliarity with sacred things comes from disconnecting the systems and structures of the church from the reality that the church is Jesus's bride. It is also due to living and ministering apart from conscious and constant dependence on the Holy Spirit and his empowering presence.

Hear Paul's command to the church:

> Do not get drunk on wine, which leads to debauchery. Instead, be filled with the Spirit, speaking to one another with psalms, hymns, and songs from the Spirit. Sing and make music from your heart to the Lord, always giving thanks to God the Father for everything, in the name of our Lord Jesus Christ. (Eph. 5:18–20)

Intimate community, genuine worship, and constant celebration flow from the church being controlled and led by the Spirit. If the church hopes to transition well to a multichurch model, it must place itself consciously and constantly under the gracious guidance of the Spirit. Scripture offers many stories of what happens when the Spirit directs the church (e.g., Acts 13:1–4; 16:6–15), and a church in the midst of a Spirit-led transition should expect the blessing of God.

Leading in the Spirit through transition begins with prayer. Too many church leaders assume this truth rather than practice it. Only a sense of complete desperation—often fostered by a transition period—will push the church to see its own inadequacies and force it onto its knees. Such desperation leading to prayerfulness should be welcomed. Moreover, transitional leadership begins with submitting the church's plan to God: "Trust in the LORD with all your heart and lean not on your own understanding; in all your ways submit to him, and he will make your paths straight" (Prov. 3:5–6). Again, a forced desperation will compel a church in transition to abandon its own inadequate plans and rely on God's wise direction. How much sweeter it is when we embrace our reliance willingly!

Final Thoughts

This chapter has focused on leading a church through a transition to a multichurch model. We have discussed four steps for navigating transition: scouting the terrain, charting a course, starting the journey, and rerouting if necessary. We have also offered three final lessons: communication degradation, working with slow adopters, and leading in the Spirit.

That's a lot of theory! But does it work? In chapter 1, we began by telling our story about coming to a point of crisis and needing a new solution. The following chapter is the rest of that story—how we became a multichurch.

12

The Rest of the Story

In chapter 1, we described the beginning of our personal journey toward becoming a multichurch. Now, in the final chapter, we look back with the benefit of some new language to describe the phases through which we passed. In the first chapter, we recounted the evolution of Sojourn Community Church as it moved (1) from pillar (one church with a single service) to gallery (one church with multiple services), and (2) from gallery to federation (one church contextualized in multiple locations). And as we stated in that first chapter, this evolution led us to a crisis. Call it a philosophical crisis or an identity crisis, but it required us to rethink how to move forward as one church comprised of multiple congregations. This last movement, (3) from federation to cooperative, is the culmination of the work—with all its trials, mistakes, and epiphanies—that comprise this book. Let's step back into the narrative with which we began.

Consolidation Phase (2011–2015)

Due in large part to Sojourn's rapid growth, the quick expansion from one to four locations, the flourishing of its many ministries and eldership, and the lack of many structures needed to sustain a church of such a size and impact, our federation model church entered into a long phase of consolidation.

In keeping with this model of multisite, Sojourn was heavily centralized, with less attention given to the particular realities and specific needs of the four congregations. From vision to finances, every facet of the organization had some level of centralized control. Along with centrally driven preaching and liturgy, a global ministry team led the vision and implementation of community groups, women's ministry, kids, youth, pastoral care, international missions, mercy, and the arts. Sojourn was the epitome of a highly controlled federation model church.

Importantly, during this consolidation phase, the percentage of the budget for central operations climbed to an average of 37 percent across four campuses, and as high as 57 percent for a particular location. On top of this number, as a part of our budget, we had a commitment of 10 percent to missions and 3 percent to long-term savings. This left 50 percent (and 30 percent in the most egregious case) of a campus's budget to remain at the campus. These campus distributions were highly controlled by the executive elders. Some locations went beyond being self-sustaining and supported the other locations, which were financially dependent on the whole. The four campuses had little input into how much support they received and how that money was to be spent.

It was around this time that we recognized the four myths we discussed in chapter 9. Of course, we realized them while dressed in sackcloth and covered in ashes. Frustration among the pastors leading the four congregations was constant. The executive elders were getting worn out from constantly defending the system, which they began to suspect was not the only way to structure Sojourn.

By God's grace this realization had been preceded by a concerted effort to strengthen the governing policies and procedures of the church. Up until this point, as we stated earlier, Sojourn was a large church of 3,500 attendees led like a church of 800. The leaders revamped the budget, articles of incorporation, and bylaws (including the statement of faith). They made savings a regular budget item. The leaders introduced mission metrics—measurements of ministry health such as attendance, auditorium capacity, participation in community groups, giving, baptisms, and membership—and provided monthly updates for the elders. The leaders instituted new policies—elder governance and grievances, whistleblower, divorce and remarriage. These measures shored up the church.

Additionally, as Sojourn lived the reality of the franchise model of multisite, it became clear that a new polity was needed. It was the move to this polity (as outlined in chapter 7) and the subsequent assessment of the organization (as outlined in chapter 6) that led to the decision to transition to a multichurch.

Sojourn as a Cooperative Multichurch (2015–present)

With a healthy polity in place, the only thing left was to reorganize the church so its operation and function were aligned with our convictions. We moved Sojourn from a federation model to a cooperative model, one church made up of multiple interdependent churches. The key reason this was done was to better reach Louisville and the surrounding metropolitan area. Using the steps laid out in chapter 11, we assessed the organization and established a transition plan. Sojourn set out on a new path.

This transition required a number of important changes to the organizational, financial, and collaborative structures of Sojourn (as laid out in chapters 6–10). As the four churches worked together, Sojourn implemented this transition over a three-year span to accommodate the needs of the staff and members and to change at a pace that was appropriate to the magnitude of the transition. In this way, Sojourn evolved from a pillar church to a multichurch over a period of fifteen years.

It seems so tidy when we package it all up in a nice little paragraph, but let's state the obvious: it was a *lot* of change. As we noted in the last chapter, most people do not readily embrace change, and we were no different. Having to overhaul the organization in so many significant areas was challenging for the leadership, staff, and members. It was messy at times, as we wrestled with making the right decisions and the right timing. It required some of our longest serving leaders to be willing to risk pursuing new opportunities. These sacrifices made it possible for us to reorganize our staff and finances, but were by no means easy decisions to make. Many of us had to sacrifice our vision of particular responsibilities and personal ministry. It was hard fought change.

We tell you this because we do not want to sugarcoat the challenge of our transformation. But we can say that Sojourn is excited for a sustainable future. Importantly, we would do it all again. Our prayer is that Sojourn's story can help your transition be a bit smoother and help you avoid some of the self-inflicted challenges that we had to undo in our last transition from federation to cooperative.

What Is Next?

Though our story is unique and will not match the stories of other churches, Sojourn's particularity can be helpful for other churches to get a glimpse into how multichurch can develop. Because churches are always evolving, we recognize that Sojourn is still a work in process. Because we find ourselves, once again, on the frontier of church models, we freely concede this is an ongoing experiment. Yet we are confident that what we have learned over the past fifteen years will be a blessing to other churches that desire to live and minister together in a multichurch model. We are still addressing the negative effects of growing in a reactive way for so many years, but the trust and excitement that come from empowerment promise a bright future.

We pray that our example, along with the principles and practices detailed in this book, can help you and your church step boldly into the future of multisite by becoming a multichurch for the transformation of your people and your city.

APPENDIX 1

Grievance Policy

What is a grievance policy?

A grievance policy gives elders of any church a clear procedure for raising concerns with the members and/or actions of the leadership council, the executive elder team, and/or the full council of elders.

The spirit of the policy

Such a policy seems unnecessary until there is disagreement or tension among the elders. Therefore, it is important for us all to consider the spirit of the policy to maintain unity (1 Peter 3:8; 1 Cor. 1:10), to pursue reconciliation (Heb. 12:13; Eph. 4:32), and to bear with one another (Col. 3:13), as long as we are able.

If we approach disagreements in such a spirit, it ought to lead to greater unity in the end. This policy intends to provide room for discourse and consideration in the event of disagreements and tensions.

A disagreement versus a charge

This policy covers only those concerns that would be categorized as disagreements rather than disqualifying sin on the part of an elder or a council. Charges of sin require an investigation and are governed by Sojourn's bylaws. This grievance police handles disagreements or tensions over an elder or a board action.

Informal

The intent of this policy is to give elders a formal procedure to share concerns but should in no way undermine the relational connections we have as elders. All members of the leadership council will adhere to an "open door policy"—willingness to discuss any and all issues—in relation to any member of the FCE. Ideally, most concerns will be noted and addressed through this informal process. If, however, an elder is not satisfied with the response and feels convicted to escalate the concern, he may do so through the formal process outlined below.

If the concern is with another elder, the basic plan of reconciliation found in Matthew 18:15–20 is the guide before entering into a formal process. Additionally, elders are encouraged to discuss their concerns with their local lead pastor (when appropriate) to seek guidance on how to proceed.

Formal

Level 1, Concern: Communicate a formal concern to the leadership council.

The purpose of formalizing a concern is to ensure that all members of the leadership council are made aware of it. This should be done only after informal efforts have been made to find resolution to the concern, without creating division among the full council of elders. A formal concern can be brought against any member of the executive elders, the leadership council, or the full council of elders. Formalization requires that the elder put his concern in writing, which will be distributed to the members of the leadership council.

Level 2, Challenge: Request a response from the leadership council.

If the concerned party is not satisfied with merely informing the leadership council, he may request a formal response. The leadership council will establish a committee to draft a formal response to the elder on its behalf. This response is intended for the concerned party but may be shared with the FCE in level 3 (below) if the concerned party is not satisfied.

Level 3, Censure: Request a "confidence vote."

> Step 1: The concerned party makes a request for a confidence vote.
>
> Step 2: The LC will post the written concern (level 1) and its formal response (level 2).
>
> Step 3: The FCE will vote to formally hear the concern. A 33 percent vote will trigger a hearing. The LC may choose to call a hearing even if the vote does not reach 33 percent.
>
> Step 4: If the FCE votes positively, a hearing will be called for the concern to be discussed and the leadership council to respond. In the event that an investigative committee is warranted, both the LC and the concerned party will approve the committee. In the case of an impasse on the makeup of the committee, each party will choose two representatives.
>
> Step 5: The FCE will give either a vote of affirmation of the elder or decision in question, or a vote of no confidence.

A vote of affirmation gives the LC the option to continue with the action or reconsider it. A vote of no confidence requires the LC to revise the decision/action and present the revision to the FCE for affirmation. In the case of a vote of no confidence of an elder, his affirmation of calling is withdrawn, requiring him to step down from his office. This withdrawal is different than disqualification. His calling may be reaffirmed through the normal elder process at the time he chooses to restart the process.

Level 4, Charge: Formal charge of disqualification or misconduct by the board.

Formal charges of disqualification or misconduct are governed by the bylaws.

APPENDIX 2

Micropolity

As we discuss in chapter 7, the polity of a multichurch has two elements: the macropolity, which deals with the leadership of the church as a whole, and the micropolity, or the leadership that takes place in the interdependent cooperative churches or the independent collective churches. This appendix focuses on this second element, or micropolity.

A multichurch has some unique challenges regarding its micropolity. Differences in church size, staffing, and leadership demand that micropolity policies be flexible enough to accommodate the various particularities of the current local churches as well as future church plants. The intent of this document is to be directional and consistent but not unduly restrictive. The goal of such policies is to help each church flourish and fulfill its mission.

As before, we present the micropolity developed at Sojourn Community Church.

Introduction

Each local church of Sojourn Community Church will establish a leadership team that is responsible for providing direction and management of the local vision. It will consist of three groups: the local leadership team (LLT), the local elder team (LET), and the local members. Together, these three groups are responsible for the execution of the mission at the local level. They will always work in collaboration with the leadership council (LC) to maintain unity with Sojourn as one church, being accountable to its overall vision.

Local Leadership Team (LLT)

The composition of the LLT is determined by the particularities of the local church. The local lead pastor is responsible for the formation and leadership of the LLT, unless otherwise specified and affirmed by the leadership council. The local elder team determines the number of members and makeup of the LLT and affirms any changes to it. The local lead pastor must submit these changes to the LC. Because the leadership council provides a form of accountability and covering for the congregation, the participation of nonstaff on the LLT is not required, nor is it discouraged. This also means that the responsibilities of governance and management do not need to be separated in the local church unless desired.

The responsibilities of the LLT are as follows:

1. Establish the local vision and particular mission, which is derivative of the larger vision of Sojourn as a whole.
2. Manage the execution of the vision and mission through the mobilization of staff, lay elders, volunteers, and members.
3. Develop key initiates and make decisions necessary for the health and growth of the local church.
4. Develop local policies in conjunction with the LET, wherever the policies of the LC have not spoken.

The deliverables of the LLT are as follows:

1. Prepare a ministry plan and submit it annually to the LC.
2. Develop an annual budget and submit it to the LC and financial accountability team.
3. Ensure that an annual review of the staff occurs.
4. Keep a written record of any significant LLT decisions (for example, capital investment, staff changes). The LLT does not need to submit this record to the LC, but should make it available upon request.

Local Lead Pastor (LLP)

The local lead pastor is responsible for the formation of the local leadership team. He builds this team based on needs for the day-to-day operation and vision development for his church. His local elder team must affirm his selections for the LLT.

The responsibilities of the LLP are as follows:

1. Formation of the LLT
2. Leadership of the LLT

Local Elder Team (LET)

The local elder team is responsible for the governance of the local church. The elders may carry out their governing responsibilities through active participation or by delegation, depending on the expression of the LLT.

The responsibilities of the LET are as follows:

1. Affirm the formation of the LLT and any changes to it.
2. Participate in the development of, and affirm, the ministry plan.
3. Participate in the development of, and affirm, the annual budget.
4. Participate in, and execute, the vision of the local church.

Local Members

The responsibilities of the local members do not change from the macropolity. They are as follows:

1. Affirm the selection of local elders.
2. Affirm the annual Sojourn-wide budget.
3. Affirm any expansion and real property transactions.
4. Affirm changes to the articles of incorporation and bylaws.
5. Participate in the vision of the church as active members.

Leadership Council (LC)

With regard to micropolity, the leadership council functions as a covering and accountability for the local churches. It provides a collaborative space for the development of local vision and goals as well as a feedback loop for the executive elders regarding the needs and vision of those churches. This feedback is essential for the growth and development of the overall vision of Sojourn. The following responsibilities of the leadership council are in particular relationship to the micropolity, and are a subset of the responsibilities of the LC with regard to Sojourn as a whole.

1. Encourage the local congregations.
2. Ensure harmony (not uniformity) between the vision of Sojourn as a whole and the vision of each congregation.
3. Review LLT structures and affirm any changes made to them.

The deliverables of the leadership council in relation to the micropolity are as follows:

1. Provide feedback for, and affirmation of, the local ministry plans.
2. Review local budgets.

Executive Elders (EE)

With regard to micropolity, the executive elders relate to the local congregation primarily through the local lead pastor. The following responsibilities of the executive elders are in particular relationship to the micropolity, and are a subset of the responsibilities of the EE with regard to Sojourn as a whole.

1. Conduct an annual performance review of the local lead pastors.
2. Promote collaboration among Sojourn churches.
3. Coach the local lead pastors for strategic development of their churches.

Church Plants (New Local Congregations)

Because most church plants (new interdependent cooperative churches or new independent collective churches) lack the depth of leadership needed to govern and manage a new congregation, established Sojourn church leaders, in conjunction with the planting pastor, will commit to supporting the launch of new works. The primary sending church is responsible for forming a temporary LLT for the church plant. This LLT will be comprised of the planting pastor and members of other Sojourn churches. That team will serve until the plant can form its own capable LLT affirmed by the LC.

Notes

Introduction

1. "Multisite revolution" reflects the title of the first book on multisite churches. See Geoff Surratt, Greg Ligon, and Warren Bird, *The Multi-Site Church Revolution: Being One Church . . . in Many Locations* (Grand Rapids, MI: Zondervan, 2006).

2. Ed Stetzer, "Multisite Churches Are Here, and Here, and Here to Stay," *The Exchange* (blog), *Christianity Today*, February 24, 2014, http://www.christianitytoday.com/edstetzer/2014/february/multisite-churches-are-here-to-stay.html.

3. Thabiti Anyabwile, "Multisite Churches Are from the Devil," *The Gospel Coalition* (blog), September 27, 2011, http://blogs.thegospelcoalition.org/thabitianyabwile/2011/09/27/multi-site-churches-are-from-the-devil/.

4. Stetzer, "Multisite Churches Are Here."

5. Warren Bird, "Now More Than 8,000 Multisite Churches," Leadership Network, February 10, 2014, http://leadnet.org/now-more-than-8000-multisite-churches/; cf. Adelle M. Banks, "Report Shows 5,000-Plus Multisite Churches," ChristianHeadlines.com, August 22, 2012, www.christianheadlines.com/news/report-shows-5-000-plus-multisite-churches.html.

6. Brad has written on the development and flourishing of community groups. See Brad House, *Community: Taking Your Small Group Off Life Support* (Wheaton, IL: Crossway, 2011).

7. Gregg R. Allison, *Sojourners and Strangers: The Doctrine of the Church* (Wheaton, IL: Crossway, 2012), 310–17.

8. For John Calvin, "Wherever we see the Word of God purely preached and heard, and the sacraments administered according to Christ's institution, there, it is not to be doubted, a church of God exists." *Institutes of the Christian Religion*, ed. John T. McNeill, trans. Ford Lewis Battles (Louisville, KY: Westminster John Knox, 2006), 4.1.9.

9. *Augsburg Confession*, 7.1–2. Available at http://bookofconcord.org/augsburgconfession.php.

10. In the tradition of evangelicalism, churches exhibit the additional distinctives of biblical authority (a commitment to the inspiration, truthfulness, sufficiency, necessity, clarity, and power of Scripture), cross-centeredness (a focus on the atoning sacrifice of Christ), mission (a devotion to call people everywhere to embrace the gospel through repentance from sin and faith in Christ), and activism (a duty to live responsibly in accordance with the gospel and to be merciful to those in need). These evangelical distinctives are developed from the Bebbington quadrilateral. David W. Bebbington, *Evangelicalism in Modern Britain: A History from the 1730s to the 1980s* (London: Unwin Hyman, 1989), 2–17.

11. Surratt, Ligon, and Bird, *The Multi-Site Church Revolution*, 18.

12. A still narrower level is conceivable, which would be a completely autonomous church that shares no connections with any other church. Such a church would not be part of a denomination, would not cooperate with other churches in a network, and would have no relationship with geographically near churches. While such completely isolated churches probably exist, we know of none and wonder about the legitimacy of calling them churches.

Chapter 1: A MultiChurch Evolution

1. The phase "paralysis by analysis" is attributed to H. Igor Ansoff, *Corporate Strategy: An Analytical Approach to Business Policy for Growth and Expansion* (New York: McGraw-Hill, 1965).

2. Milton Friedman, *Capitalism and Freedom*, 40th anniversary ed. (Chicago: University of Chicago Press, 1982), ix.

Section 1: Scouting

1. US Army, *The Infantry Reconnaissance Platoon and Squad (Airborne, Air Assault, Light Infantry)* FM 7–92 (Washington, DC: Government Printing Office, 2001).

Chapter 2: Landscape

1. The Greek phrase *kat oikon* is best rendered "from house to house" (NASB, CSB, KJV, and NKJV). Other renditions such as "in their homes" (ESV, NIV) miss the distributive sense: the church of Jerusalem, in addition to gathering in the temple, fanned out "in the *various* homes" (BAG, 1st ed.), thus gathering "from house to house."

2. Despite this clear evidence that the church in Jerusalem was multisite, some critics continue to assert, "There's no clear example of a multi-site church in the New Testament, only supposition. 'Well, surely, the Christians in a city could not have all met . . .' (but see Acts 2:46; 5:12; 6:2)" (Jonathan Leeman, "Twenty-Two Problems with Multi-Site Churches," *9Marks*, September 30, 2014, https://9marks.org/article/twenty-two-problems-with-multi-site-churches/). The Jerusalem church was indeed multisite, and the issue was not whether all

the believers could meet in the temple. They clearly could and did meet in this location. Rather, Luke narrates that these believers daily met together in the disciples' homes, where they continued to do in separate locations what they did in the one location.

3. Paul offers greetings from this same church meeting in the home of Aquila and Priscilla to the Corinthian Christians (1 Cor. 16:19).

4. Another possible example is the city of Colossae, in which the church met in the home of Philemon (Philem. 2). This location may have been the only gathering of the Colossian church, or it may have been one of several.

5. This pattern addresses another critique of multisite: "If a church is constituted by the preaching of the Word and the distribution of the ordinances under the binding authority of the keys, every 'campus' where those activities transpire is actually a church. 'Multi-site church' is a misnomer. It's a collection of churches under one administration." But the church in Jerusalem was not a collection of churches in which its many members, distributed into the disciples' houses, met regularly. In those homes, where the Word was preached, prayers were voiced, money was given sacrificially, the Lord's Supper was celebrated, and more, the church of Jerusalem assembled to worship. The church—not the churches—of Jerusalem gathered in these many locations. (Jonathan Leeman, "Twenty-Two Problems with Multi-Site Churches.")

6. Gary L. McIntosh, *Make Room for the Boom . . . or Bust: Six Models for Reaching Three Generations* (Grand Rapids, MI: Fleming H. Revel, 1997), 138–40. In 1981, Scott Memorial Baptist Church was renamed Shadow Mountain Community Church and David Jeremiah became its pastor.

7. Mount Paran North became an autonomous church in 1997, and in 2012 it launched its second site, Mount Paran North Canton. See https://www .mtparan.com/default.aspx?page=8510.

8. S. David Moore, "Jack W. Hayford, Jr., A Spiritual Biography" (PhD diss., Regent University, 2008), 199–200.

9. Randy Pope, "3 Reasons We Stopped Doing Multisite Church," *Christianity Today* (Summer 2015), 58–59. As the title underscores, Perimeter Church is no longer multisite but engages in church planting throughout the Atlanta region.

10. Russell Chandler, *Racing toward 2001: The Forces Shaping America's Religious Future* (Grand Rapids, MI: Zondervan, 1992), 243.

11. Brian Nathaniel Frye, "The Multi-Site Church Phenomenon in North America: 1950–2010" (PhD diss., Southern Baptist Theological Seminary, 2011), 100.

12. The early 1990s also witnessed the advent of serious discussion about this phenomenon, including definitions (e.g., "extended geographic parish churches"; "the untethered church") and descriptions of various types of multisite realities. Elmer Towns, *An Inside Look at 10 of Today's Most Innovative Churches: What They're Doing, How They're Doing It, and How You Can Apply Their Ideas to Your Church* (Ventura, CA: Regal, 1990), 236–37; Bill Easum and Dave Travis,

Beyond the Box: Innovative Churches That Work (Loveland, CO: Group, 2003), 85–96; Lyle Schaller, *Innovations in Ministry: Models for the 21st Century* (Nashville: Abingdon, 1994), 121. For further discussion, see Frye, "The Multi-Site Church Phenomenon," 2–4.

13. Indeed, in 1999 J. Timothy Allen and J. V. Thomas wrote *One Church, Many Congregations: The Key Church Strategy* (Nashville: Abingdon, 1999), which encouraged churches to start new congregations: "The Key Church Strategy is an evangelism strategy. One church starts other congregations primarily composed of a particular ethnic or cultural group, which may or may not remain a part of the one Key Church." Allen and Thomas, two Southern Baptists, developed the Key Church Strategy that was implemented in over 150 Southern Baptist churches in Texas. Appendix 2 of their book recounts case studies of multisite churches throughout the US.

14. Warren Bird, "Survey of 1,000 Multi-Site Churches: A Dozen of the Most Significant Findings," Leadership Network, www.leadnet.org; and Dave Ferguson, "The Multi-Site Movement: A New and Effective Way to Reach More People for Christ," *Christianity Today*, http://www.christianitytoday.com/global/printer.html?/bcl/areas/vision-strategy/articles/102605.html.

15. Surratt, Ligon, and Bird, *The Multi-Site Church Revolution*; and *The Multi-Site Church Road Trip: Exploring the New Normal* (Grand Rapids, MI: Zondervan, 2009).

16. According to the Leadership Network/Generis Multisite Church Scorecard. See Warren Bird, "Now More Than 8,000 Multisite Churches."

17. Stetzer, "Multisite Churches Are Here."

18. Frye, "The Multi-Site Church Phenomenon," 116.

19. Frank L. Smith, "What Is Worship?" in *Worship in the Presence of God*, ed. Frank L. Smith and David C. Lachman (Greenville, SC: Greenville Seminary Press, 1992), 16–17.

20. Some of this discussion is taken from Gregg R. Allison, *Sojourners and Strangers*, 310–17.

21. Mark Dever, *The Church: The Gospel Made Visible* (Nashville: B&H Academic, 2012), 133. The original does not have the macron over the *e*. It has been added here for precision.

22. Ibid., 136.

23. Pliny, *Letter 10, to Trajan*, 46, in *Documents of the Christian Church*, ed. Henry Bettenson and Chris Maunder, 3rd ed. (Oxford: Oxford University Press, 1999), 4; *Didache*, 14, in *Ante-Nicene Fathers*, ed. Alexander Roberts et al., 10 vols. (Peabody, MA.: Hendrickson, 1994), 7:381; Justin Martyr, *First Apology*, 67, in *ANF*, 1:186.

24. Dever, *The Church*, 137.

25. Gk.: ὅλη ἡ ἐκκλησία, or *holē hē ekklēsia*.

26. What are the implications of the early church practice of the celebration of the Lord's Supper, specifically, the practice of sending the deacons, after

the conclusion of the service, with the elements of the Supper to the church members who were absent? If "church" refers to the assembly of the members, and these absent members were not gathered together with the present members, why would they be considered to be part of the church and included in the participation in this sacred meal? Justin Martyr, *First Apology*, 65, in *ANF*, 1:185.

27. Augustine, *On Baptism, Against the Donatists*, 5.27, 38, in *NPNF*, 4:477.

28. Some of this discussion is taken from Allison, *Sojourners and Strangers*, 310–17.

29. John Piper, "Treasuring Christ Together as a Church on Multiple Campuses," November 4, 2007, http://www.desiringgod.org/messages/treasuring-christ-together-as-a-church-on-multiple-campuses. See especially the letter written by Piper to his church three years prior on April 21, 2004: "Treasuring Christ Together: A Vision for Church Planting and Campus Multiplication, Bethlehem Baptist Church, 2004–2014."

30. This section summarizes Frye, "The Multi-Site Church Phenomenon," 265–74.

31. Ibid., 274–79, 289–91.

Chapter 3: Landmarks

1. Nik Ripken with Gregg Lewis, *The Insanity of God: A True Story of Faith Resurrected* (Nashville: B&H, 2013), 219.

2. Thom Rainer, "Seven Trends in Worship Service Times," ThomRainer.com, May 25, 2015, http://thomrainer.com/2015/05/seven-trends-in-worship-service-times/.

3. 9Marks is a network of churches that are characterized by preaching, biblical theology, the gospel, conversion, evangelism, membership, discipline, discipleship, and leadership. See https://9marks.org.

4. According to a 2015 study by the Hartford Institute for Religious Research, 58 percent of US churches have less than one hundred people in attendance at their Sunday worship service. Indeed, the median attendance is eighty people.

5. In most books and articles that offer reasons for churches dying, one reason is that the church becomes internally rather than externally focused.

6. Bird, "Now More than 8,000 Multisite Churches."

7. Thom Rainer, "Seven Trends in Worship Service Times."

8. "Worship Options," NorthCoastChurch.com, www.northcoastchurch.com/locations/vista-campus/worship-options/. North Coast Church also serves as an example of a franchise model multisite church as it has, in addition to its Vista location (a gallery model), four other campuses in San Diego. Each campus views the same sermon via video but has a campus pastor and a full variety of ministries.

9. Timothy Keller, *Center Church: Doing Balanced, Gospel-Centered Ministry in Your City* (Grand Rapids, MI: Zondervan, 2012), 89.

10. Gregg R. Allison, *The Baker Compact Dictionary of Theological Terms* (Grand Rapids, MI: Baker, 2016), 48.

11. The Gospel Coalition, "Vision," *Foundational Documents*, III.3, https://www.thegospelcoalition.org/about/foundation-documents/vision.

12. Sean Mortenson, "The Mission and Structure of Redemption Church," Redemption Church, January 21, 2016, http://www.redemptionaz.com/missionandstructure/.

13. Ibid.

14. Ibid.

15. Dave Harvey, "What Is a Network?," lecture, Sojourn Network Pastors' Retreat, May 2015.

Chapter 4: Landmines

1. It is highly desirable that objections to and criticisms of multisite be based on empirical evidence, careful observation, and significant research rather than guesses or suppositions as to what these churches are. An example of what happens when this common courtesy is neglected is the exchange between Ed Stetzer (who voiced questions and cautions about multisite) and Geoff Surratt (who voiced concerns about Stetzer's lack of evidence about multisite, as revealed in Stetzer's line of questioning). Ed Stetzer, "Questions for 'Questions for McChurch,'" *The Exchange* (blog), *Christianity Today*, June 5, 2008, http://www.christianitytoday.com/edstetzer/2008/june/questions-for-questions-for-mcchurch.html.

2. This point is well made by Scott Thumma and Dave Travis, *Beyond Megachurch Myths: What We Can Learn from America's Largest Churches* (San Francisco: Jossey-Bass, 2007), 55–78.

3. For discussion of the call, character, and competency of pastors, see Allison, *Sojourners and Strangers*, 211–23; also, Alexander Strauch, *Biblical Eldership*, rev. ed. (Colorado Springs, CO: Lewis and Roth, 2003).

4. For further discussion, see Matt Rogers, "The Terrifying Danger of Falling Off My Own Platform," *The Blazing Center* (blog), July 18, 2016, http://theblazingcenter.com/2016/07/the-terrifying-danger-of-falling-off-my-own -platform.html.

5. At the same time, it is good to remember that the "writing" apostles expressed their preference for personal contact with the recipients of their letters (Rom. 1:10–11; 2 John 12; 3 John 13–14).

6. Personal conversation with Scott Allen.

7. Jonathan Leeman, "Twenty-Two Problems with Multi-Site Churches."

8. Jamus Howell Edwards II, "Leadership Structures and Dynamics in Multisite Churches: A Quantitative Study" (PhD diss., Southern Baptist Theological Seminary, 2016), 177–78.

9. See, for example, Mike Wilkerson's ministry at www.redemptiongroups.com and his *Redemption: Freed by Jesus from the Idols We Worship and the Wounds We Carry* (Wheaton: Crossway, 2011). He carried out this intense and important ministry as pastor at Mars Hill.

10. Thomas White and John Mark Yeats, *Franchising McChurch: Feeding Our Obsession with Easy Christianity* (Colorado Springs, CO: David C. Cook, 2009).

11. Thabiti Anyabwile, "Multi-Site Churches Are from the Devil."

12. Thomas White, "Nine Reasons Why I Do Not Like Multisite," *9Marks* 6, no. 3 (2009), https://9marks.org/article/nine-reasons-i-dont-multi-site-churches/.

13. The subject of a forthcoming Ph.D. dissertation by Hans Googer at Southern Baptist Theological Seminary.

14. Greg Gilbert acknowledges that this criticism of such multisite churches is inaccurate. "There is something distinctly congregational about the way these churches conduct themselves." He also makes the distinction between elder-ruled churches and elder-led churches. Greg Gilbert, "What Is This Thing Anyway? A Multi-site Taxonomy," *9Marks* 6, no. 3 (2009), https://9marks.org/article/what-thing-anyway-multi-site-taxonomy/.

15. For development of these four areas of elder responsibilities, see Allison, *Sojourners and Strangers*, 211–23.

16. Ibid., 242–47.

17. This objection is directed at a certain version of multisite, one in which the lead pastor exercises absolute control over the decisions and preaches all the time to all the members through his sermons being broadcast to all the campuses. Because of these activities, "the multisite methodology forms mini-dioceses. The head pastor serves as the 'virtual' bishop, the founding location as the headquarters, and the locations as the affiliated members." In such an episcopalian structure, the "local congregation has no control. In function, the multi-campus church is like a hierarchical McDenomination that dictates what each franchise must do" (Thomas White, "Nine Reasons Why I Do Not Like Multisite"). A multisite church governed this way is not congregational, but episcopalian.

    This criticism is wrong for at least two reasons: First, no actual multisite church reflects this description of absolute authority exercised by its lead pastor, or bishop, as Jamus Edwards demonstrates (Edwards, "Leadership Structures and Dynamics in Multisite Churches," 46n80). Accordingly, the objection is a phantom and thus pointless. Second, the critique misunderstands the nature of episcopalian government. In the episcopalian structure, ultimate authority does indeed reside in the bishop, but there are other authoritative leaders—presbyters/elders/priests and deacons—in the church. Importantly, bishops are accountable to other bishops, so they cannot just do whatever they please. Moreover, episcopalianism does not envision any authority for church members. But multisite churches that are congregational do include a significant, authoritative role for members. Thus, the charge that multisite is episcopalian fails.

18. A second governance objection is that multisite churches are actually presbyterian in government, not congregational as they claim. Refusing to accept that the various campuses are actually the congregations of one church, this objection understands them to be separate churches: a multisite church consisting of four campuses is in fact four independent churches. If this is the case, then when the elders of one of the congregations meet concerning their congregation, they function legitimately. Like the session in the presbyterian

system, the elders exercise authority in their areas of responsibility for their congregation. However, when all the elders of the various congregations gather for prayer and decisions about vision, philosophy of ministry, budget, starting a new site, and so forth—matters concerning all four of the congregations—they compose a type of presbytery. This presbytery, then, is an authoritative governing structure above the local church level: it makes authoritative determinations for the separate churches. This presbyterian governing structure runs counter to congregationalism and its insistence that there can be no such governance above that of the local church. The four independent churches have the responsibility to make those authoritative decisions about vision, ministry, budget, and more, for themselves. And they cannot concede them to a higher board consisting of the elders from those four churches.

But if, as argued previously, there is biblical precedent for one church that meets in various locations, then the insistence that the four congregations are actually separate churches simply misses the point. On this matter, proponents and opponents of multisite are like ships passing each other in the night.

Additionally, the objection misunderstands the nature of presbyterian government. In this structure, ultimate authority resides in the elders as representatives of the church. On a local church level, elders compose a *session*: this governing body has the responsibility and authority to make decisions for its local church. The elders from the local churches in a geographical area (e.g., the city of Boston) form a *presbytery*: this governing body has the responsibility and authority to make decisions for all those local churches. The elders from the presbyteries in a broader region (e.g., the state of Massachusetts) form a *synod*; this governing body has the responsibility and authority to make decisions for all the churches in that region/state. In some presbyterian denominations, an even higher body—the *general assembly*—has the responsibility and authority to make decisions for all the churches in a nation. Significantly, no actual expression of multisite even comes close to resembling this presbyterian governance structure.

Importantly, and in contrast with multisite churches that are congregational, presbyterianism does not envision any authority for church members. They are represented by their elders in various authoritative structures, both at the local church level (the session) and at broader levels (the presbytery, the synod, and the general assembly). But church members (those who are not elders) do not have authority themselves. However, multisite churches that are congregational do include a significant, authoritative role for members. Thus, the charge that multisite is presbyterian fails.

19. For example, this concern is raised by Elmer Towns, Ed Stetzer, and Warren Bird in *11 Innovations in the Local Church: How Today's Leaders Can Learn, Discern and Move into the Future* (Ventura, CA: Regal, 1995), 65–94.

20. Surratt, Ligon, and Bird, *The Multi-Site Church Revolution*, 10.

21. This reality contradicts the unfounded claim that few proponents of multisite

have considered the phenomenon from a scriptural perspective. White and Yeats, *Franchising McChurch*, 172.

22. See Jonathan Leeman, "Twenty-Two Problems with Multi-Site Churches." Thomas White also charges multisite with creating "an un-gathered 'church'" that consequently "cannot know one another, love one another, or bear one another's burdens in the same way a single assembly can." If the criticism is that all the 1,800 members of a multisite church can't know all the other 1,800 members so as to love them and bear their burdens, the charge is certainly true. But the same problem arises in any church with more than a couple hundred people. So, when applied to the church in Jerusalem, how would it be possible that the 3,000 (which quickly expanded to more than 5,000) new believers knew all the other believers so as to care and serve one another? Would not such personal, loving relationships primarily take place as portions of these new Christians gathered in the disciples' houses? As such care and service was exemplified in the church of Jerusalem, so it can be, and is, carried out in multisite churches today. See Thomas White, "Nine Reasons I Do Not Like Multisite."

23. Frye, "The Multi-Site Church Phenomenon," 229.

24. Ibid., 230.

Chapter 5: The Future

1. Colin Marshall and Tony Payne, *The Trellis and the Vine* (Kingsford NSW, Australia: Matthias Media, 2009).

2. Emphasis added.

3. Te-Li Lau, "Ephesians," *NIV Zondervan Study Bible*, ed. D. A. Carson (Grand Rapids, MI: Zondervan, 2015), 2402.

4. Some of this discussion is taken from Allison, *Sojourners and Strangers*, 168–78.

5. Dietrich Bonhoeffer, *Life Together*, trans. Daniel W. Bloesch and James H. Burtness (Minneapolis, MN: Fortress, 2004), 19.

6. Andy Crouch, *Strong and Weak: Embracing the Life of Love, Risk & True Flourishing* (Downers Grove, IL: IVP Books, 2016), 117 and 172.

7. Bonhoeffer, *Life Together*, 23.

8. For further discussion, see the section on contextualization in chapter 3.

9. Jim Collins, *Good to Great: Why Some Companies Make the Leap ... And Others Don't* (New York: HarperCollins, 2001), and Richard Koch and Gregory Lockwood, *Simplify: How the Best Businesses in the World Succeed* (Irvine, CA: Entrepreneur, 2016).

10. For example, Thom S. Rainer and Eric Geiger, *Simple Church: Returning to God's Process for Making Disciples* (Nashville: B&H, 2011).

11. Sinclair B. Ferguson, *Grow in Grace* (Edinburgh: Banner of Truth, 1989), 67.

Chapter 6: MultiOrg

1. From a conversation with Lyle Wells, Flippen Group.

2. Jim Collins, *How the Mighty Fall: And Why Some Companies Never Give In* (New York: HarperCollins, 2009), stage 2.

3. For example: Ichak Adizes, *Corporate Lifecycles: How and Why Corporations Grow and Die and What to Do about It* (Paramus, NJ: Prentice Hall, 1988); John Brothers and Anne Sherman, *Building Nonprofit Capacity: A Guide to Managing Change through Organizational Lifecycles* (San Francisco: Jossey-Bass, 2012); Paul Connolly, *Navigating the Organizational Lifecycle: A Capacity-Building Guide for Nonprofit Leaders* (Washington, DC: BoardSource, 2006).

4. House, *Community*, 71–72.

5. Ori Brafman and Rod A. Beckstrom, *The Starfish and the Spider: The Unstoppable Power of Leaderless Organizations* (New York: Penguin, 2006).

6. Noam Wasserman, "The Founder's Dilemma," *Harvard Business Review*, February 2008, https://hbr.org/2008/02/the-founders-dilemma.

7. Wasserman notes that exceptions to this rule, such as Bill Gates, exist but are rare.

8. The following chart is adapted from Charles E. Hummel, *Tyranny of the Urgent*, rev. ed. (Downers Grove, IL: InterVarsity, 1994).

9. Lesslie Newbigin, *The Open Secret: An Introduction to the Theology of Mission* (Grand Rapids, MI: Eerdmans, 1995), 1.

10. House, *Community*, 66. His reference is to Ed Stetzer, "Missional Missiology," lecture series, Mars Hill Church, in Seattle, WA, on November 13–14, 2009.

11. Interestingly, multichurch models are experimenting with launching new interdependent churches (cooperative model) and new independent churches that collaborate together (the collaborative model) with a view toward umbilical (not unbiblical!) church planting. Some proponents call this strategy *runway planting* or *phased planting*. That is, the new churches are closely tied to the whole church for their initial years, and as they become self-sustaining, mature, multiplying churches, they become more independent and responsible as sending agencies for the mission of God.

Chapter 7: MultiPolity

1. Paul Tripp, "Mars Hill BoAA Statement," August 12, 2014, http://www.paultripp.com/articles/posts/mars-hill-boaa-statement.

2. Some may object that the makeup of the LC does not meet the standards of board independence (see http://www.ecfa.org/Content/Comment2). However, with all due respect to ECFA, we believe its standards are more suited for nonprofit organizations than they are for the complexities of a church, as leadership requires calling as much as competency. As explained earlier, we strongly advise against external boards that meet the standard of board independence but are significantly less capable of providing the accountability found in our redemptive polity.

3. The lead pastor representative cannot be a member of the EE. Mission metrics consist of data and statistics (for example, attendance, community groups,

baptisms) collected from each local church and complied into a dashboard for use by the EE, LC, and FCE.

4. Strauch, *Biblical Eldership*, 45–50.

Chapter 8: MultiMinistry

1. Brenda Naomi Rosenberg and Samia M. Bahsoun, *Harnessing the Power of Tension* (n.p.: Tectonic Leadership Center, 2015).
2. One of many lessons we learned from Redemption Church, Phoenix, Arizona.
3. Edward Hess, "Creating an Innovation Culture: Accepting Failure Is Necessary," *Forbes*, June 20, 2012, http://www.forbes.com/sites/darden/2012/06/20/ creating-an-innovation-culture-accepting-failure-is-necessary/#3e71f49c4e19.
4. Ibid.

Chapter 9: MultiMoney

1. Christoph Roser, "Cost of Complexity," AllAboutLean.com, April 27, 2014, http://www.allaboutlean.com/cost-of-complexity/; and Stephen A. Wilson and Andrei Perumal, "A Fresh Take on Complexity Costs," American Management Association, http://www.amanet.org/training/articles/A-Fresh-Take-on -Complexity-Costs.aspx.
2. These percentages do not include dollars designated for missions. Many churches designate another 10 percent of their budget for international missions, church planting, and, in some cases, mercy projects.
3. By God's grace the majority of this transition was accomplished by the transition of some senior leaders to new and significant works, the reassignment of central staff to local positions, and a reduction in a small number of staff.

Chapter 11: Navigating Transition

1. For an example of the phenomenon of selective-memory nostalgia in post– World War II America, see Yuval Levin, *The Fractured Republic: Renewing America's Social Contract in the Age of Individualism* (New York: Basic Books, 2016).
2. Ronald A. Heifetz and Marty Linsky, *Leadership on the Line: Staying Alive through the Dangers of Leading* (Cambridge, MA: Harvard Business Review Press, 2002).
3. Ibid., 13.
4. Ibid.
5. Ibid., 27.
6. Ibid. See also W. Wayne Burke, *Organizational Change: Theory and Practice* (Thousand Oaks, CA: Sage Publications, 2013); John P. Kotter, *Leading Change*, 1st rev. ed. (Cambridge, MA: Harvard Business Review Press, 2012); Barbara Senior and Stephen Swailes, *Organizational Change*, 5th ed. (New York: Pearson, 2016).

7. Simon Sinek, *Start with Why: How Great Leaders Inspire Everyone to Take Action* (New York: Portfolio/Penguin, 2009), 41.

8. Collins, *Good to Great*, 41.

9. Heifetz and Linsky, *Leadership on the Line*, ch. 3.

10. Sinek, *Start with Why*, 227.

11. Heifetz and Linsky, *Leadership on the Line*, ch. 4.

12. Elliot Grudem, notes from "Leaders Collective" (Raleigh, NC, April 19, 2016).